THIS BOOK
BELONGS TO

Copyright

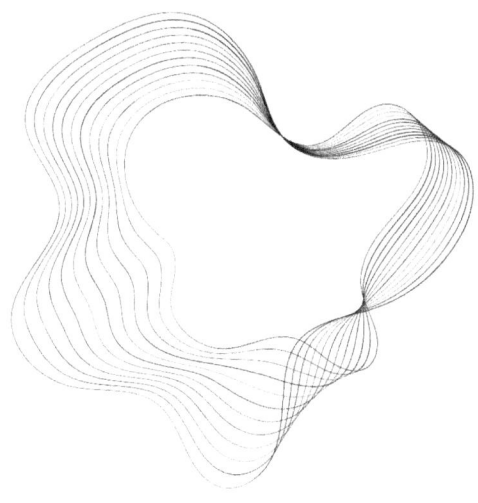

"Haunted Realms"
"Fantastic Faces and Medieval Nature"

Alberto Mario Montoya Tamayo

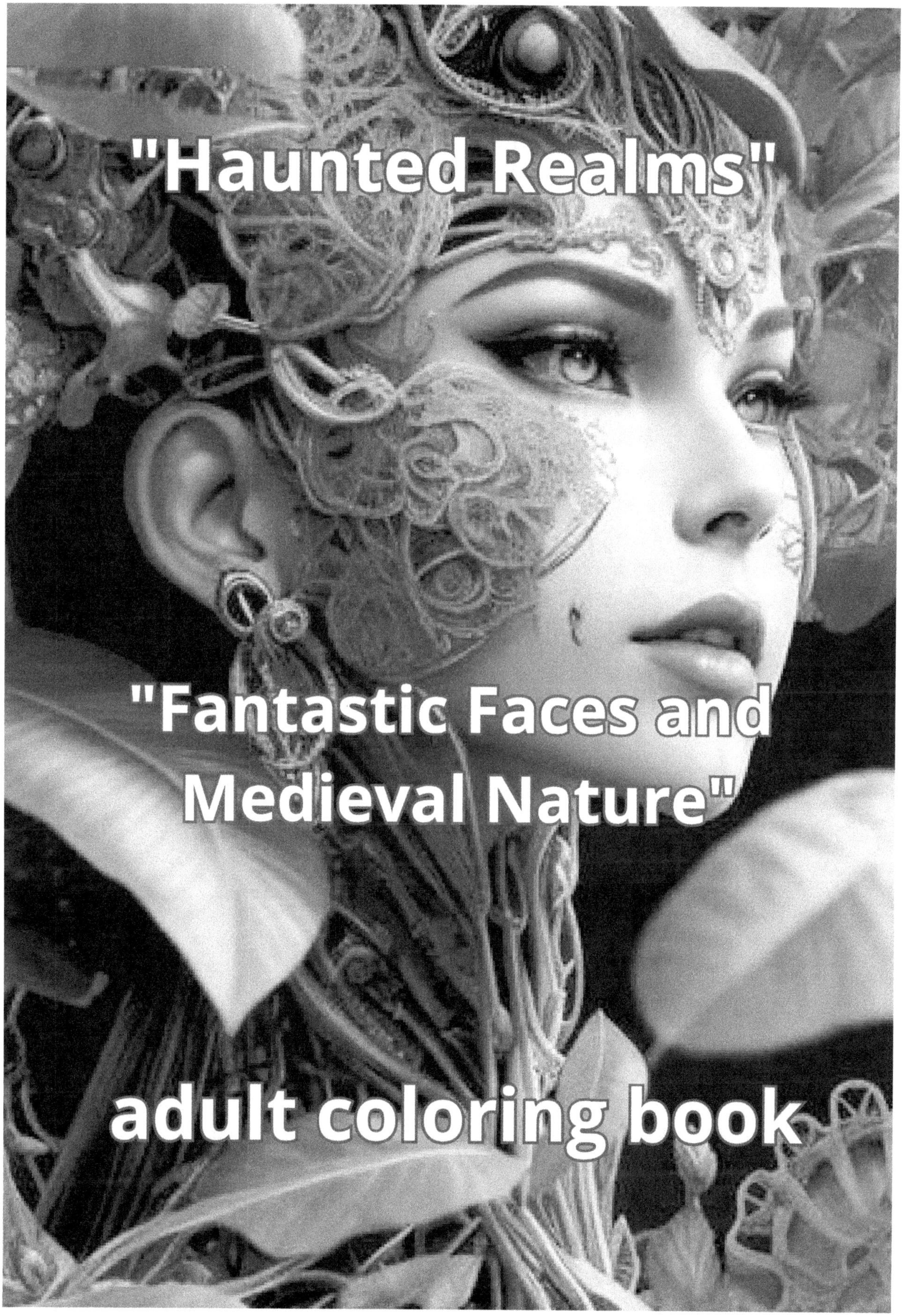
"Haunted Realms"
"Fantastic Faces and Medieval Nature"
adult coloring book

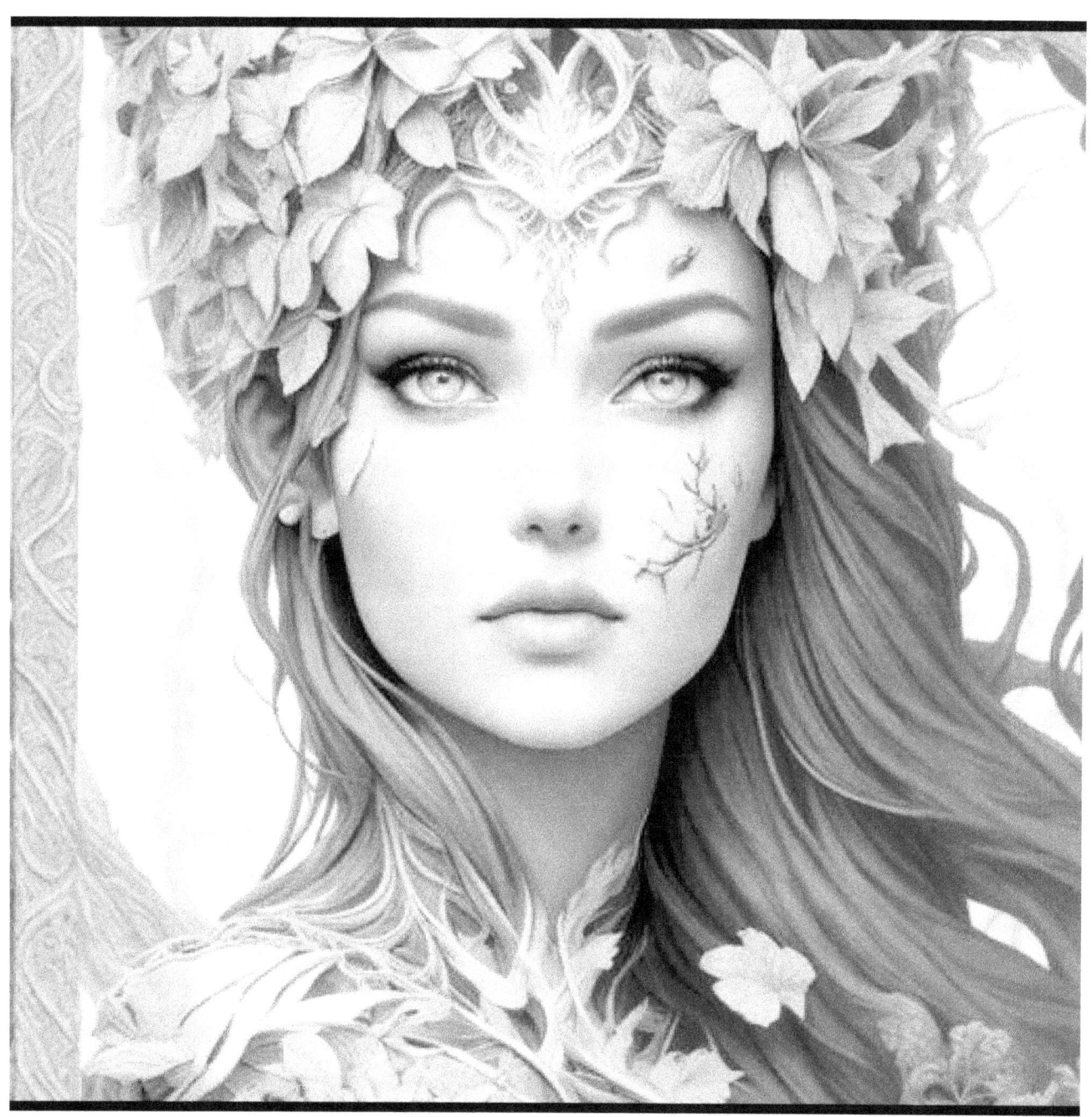

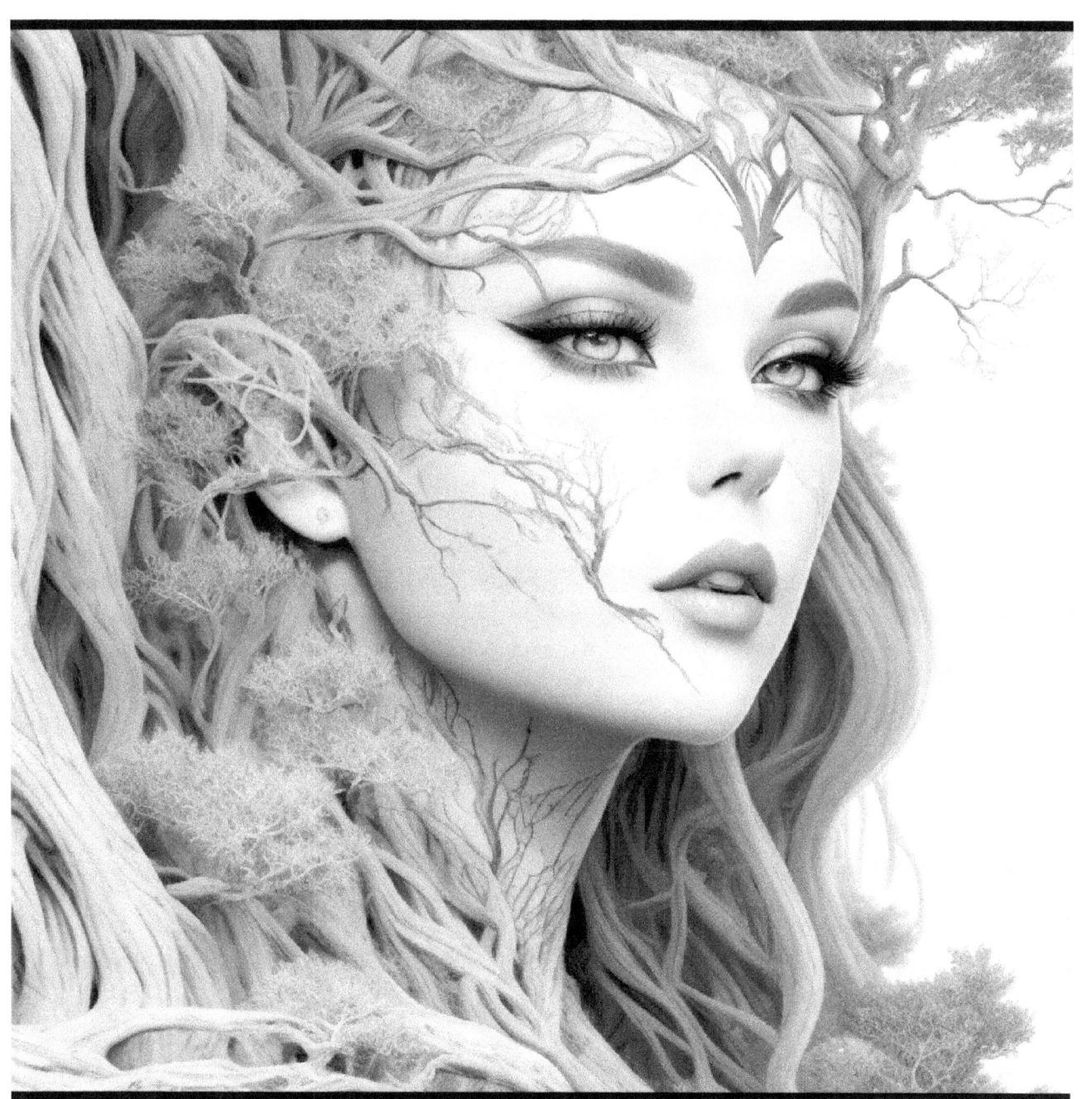

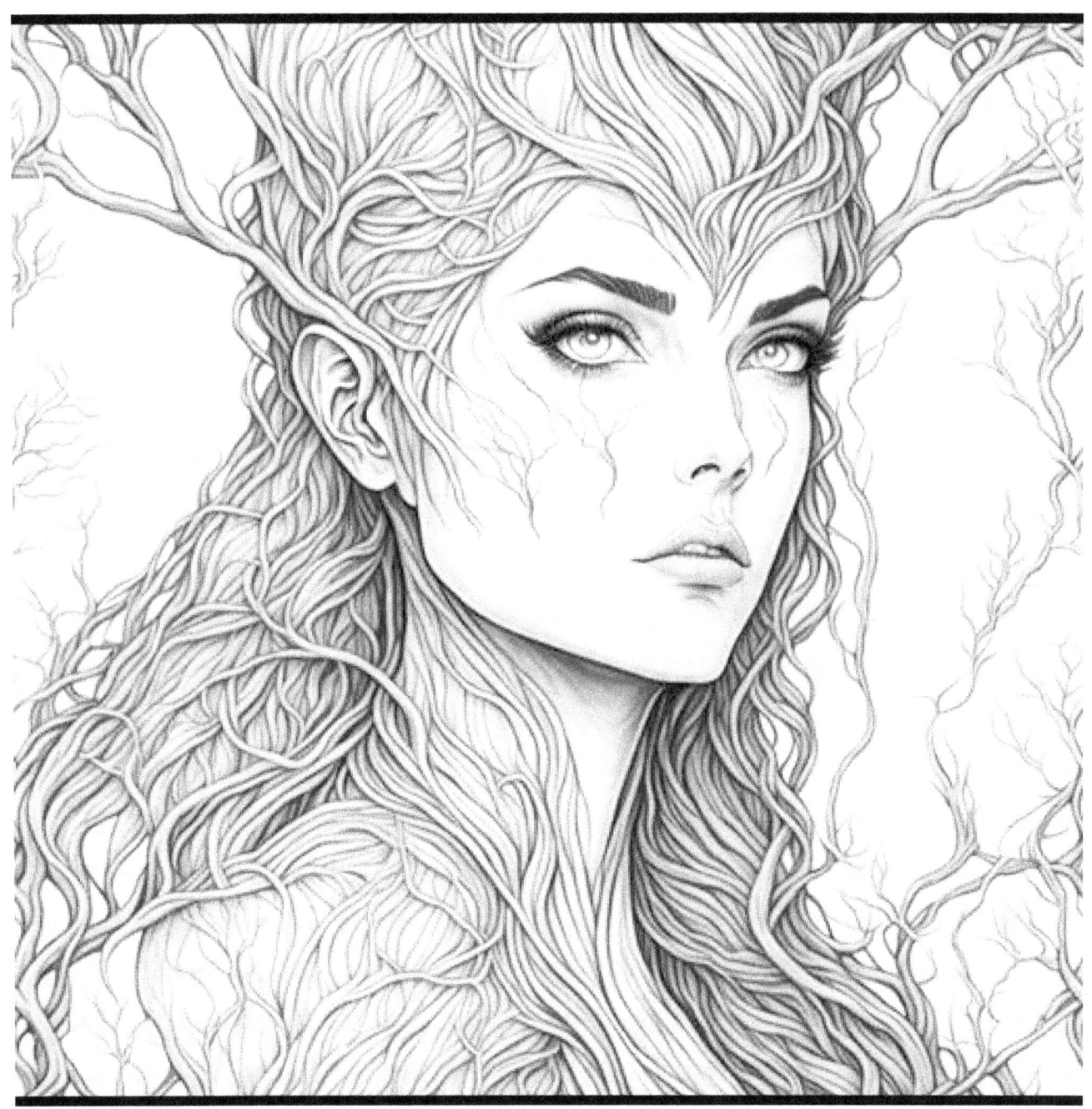

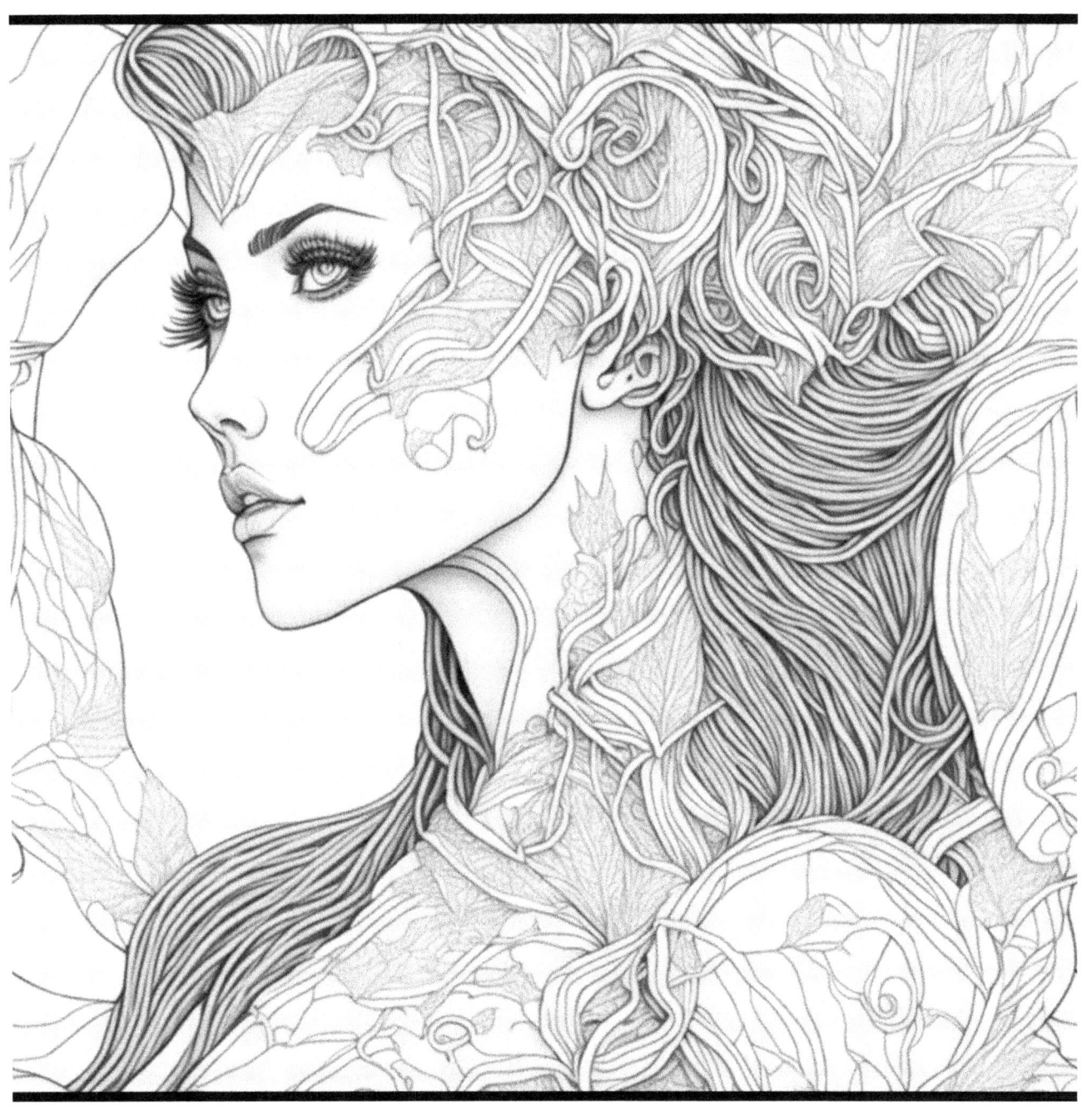

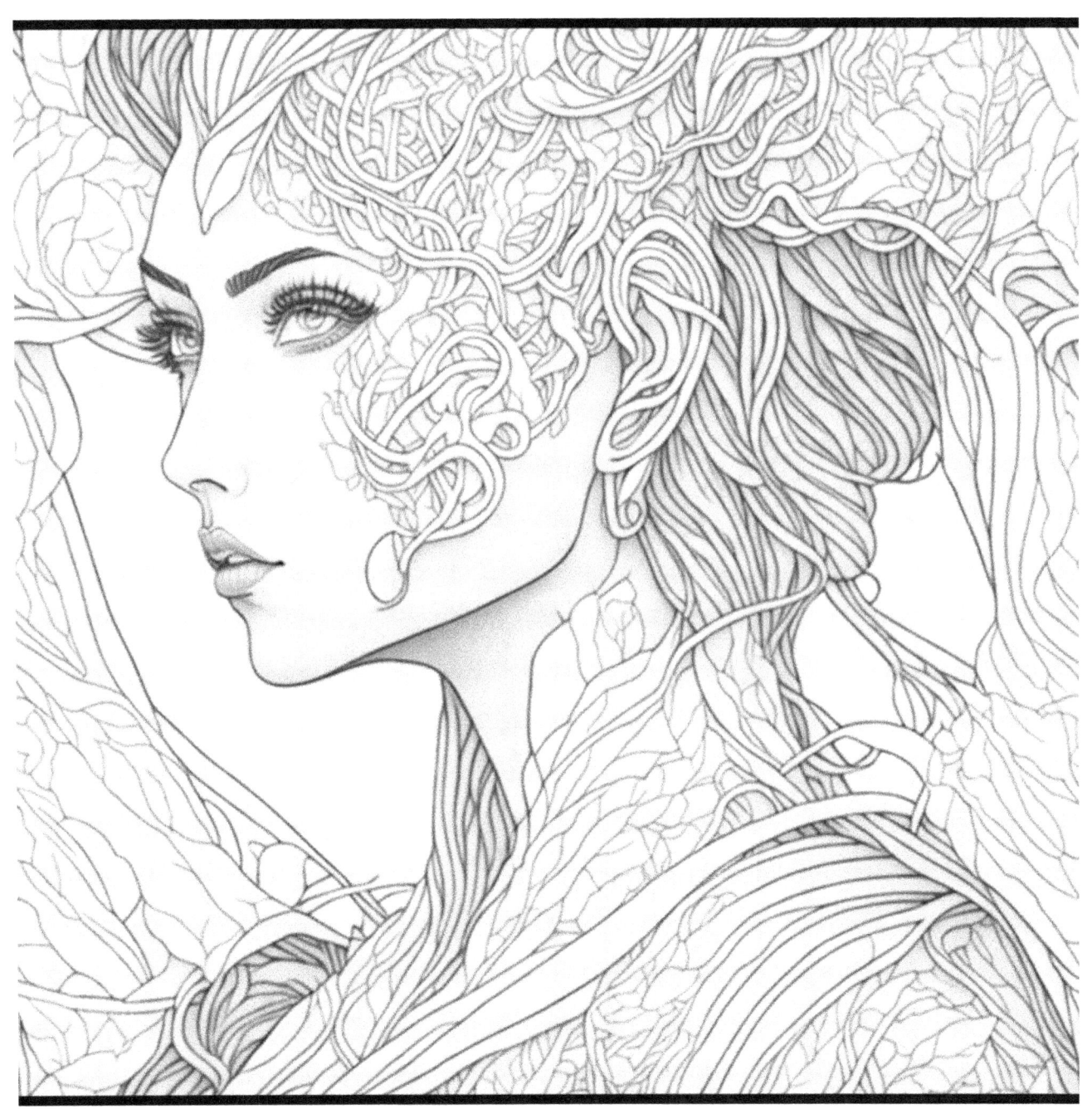

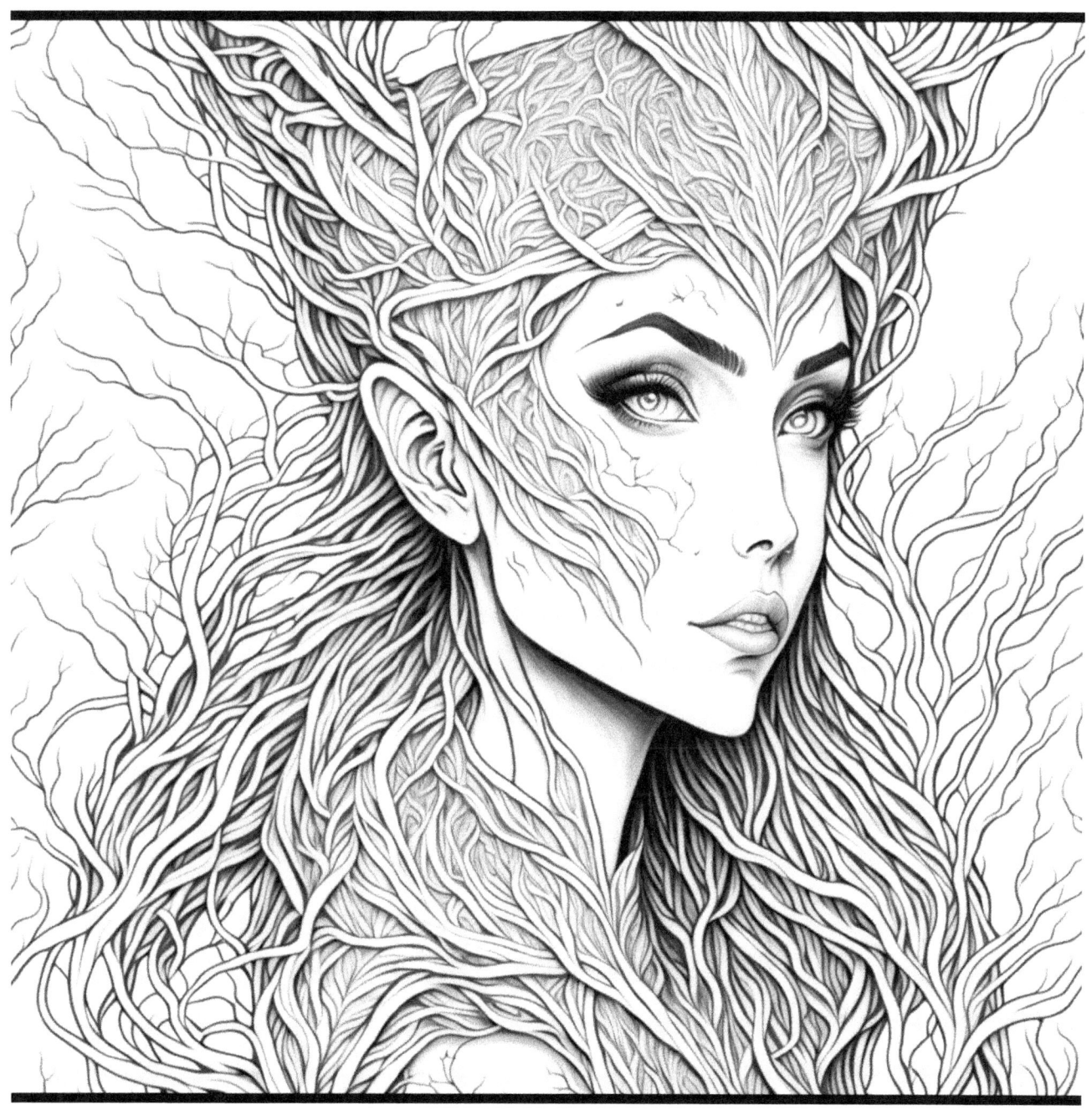

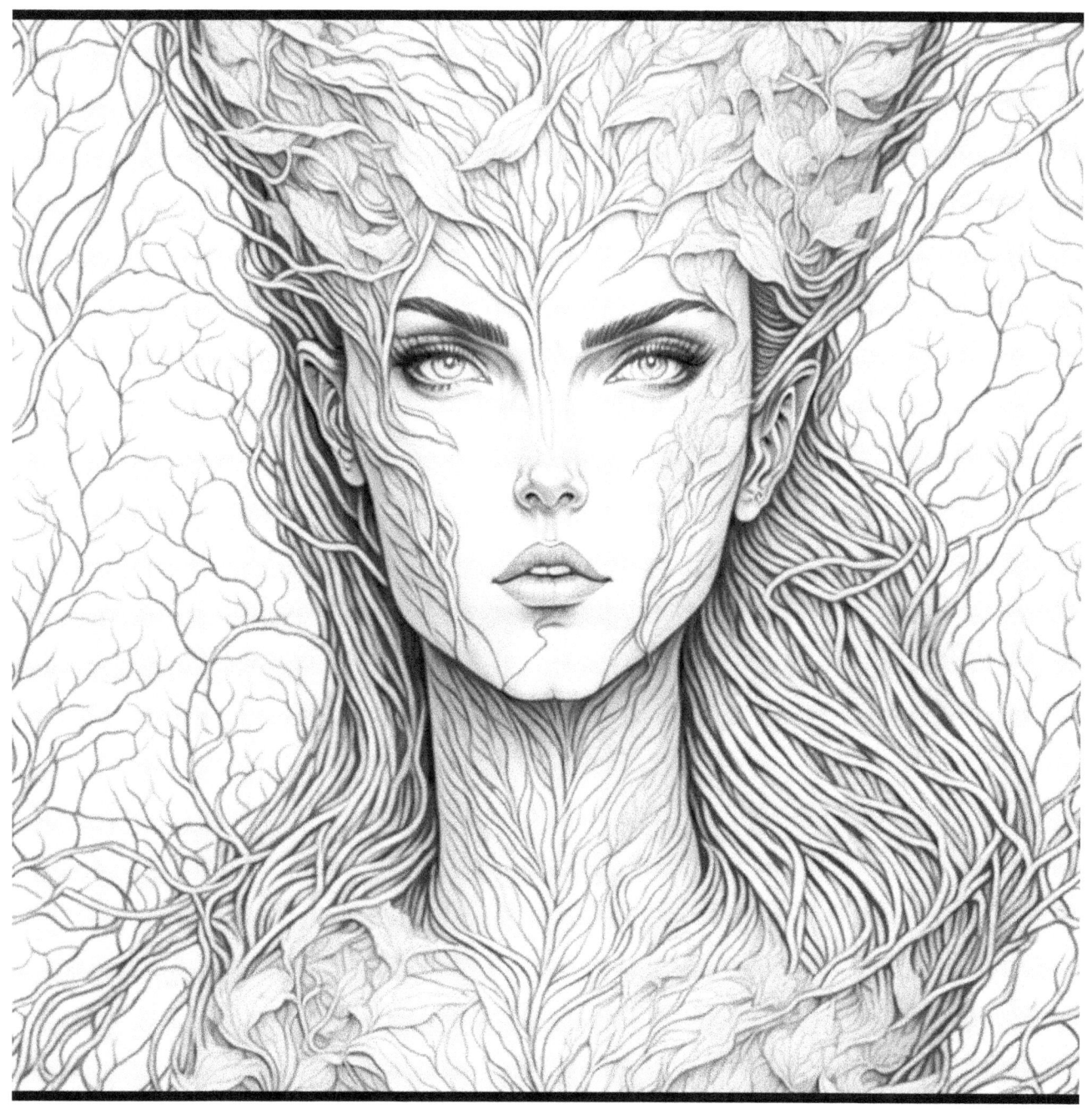

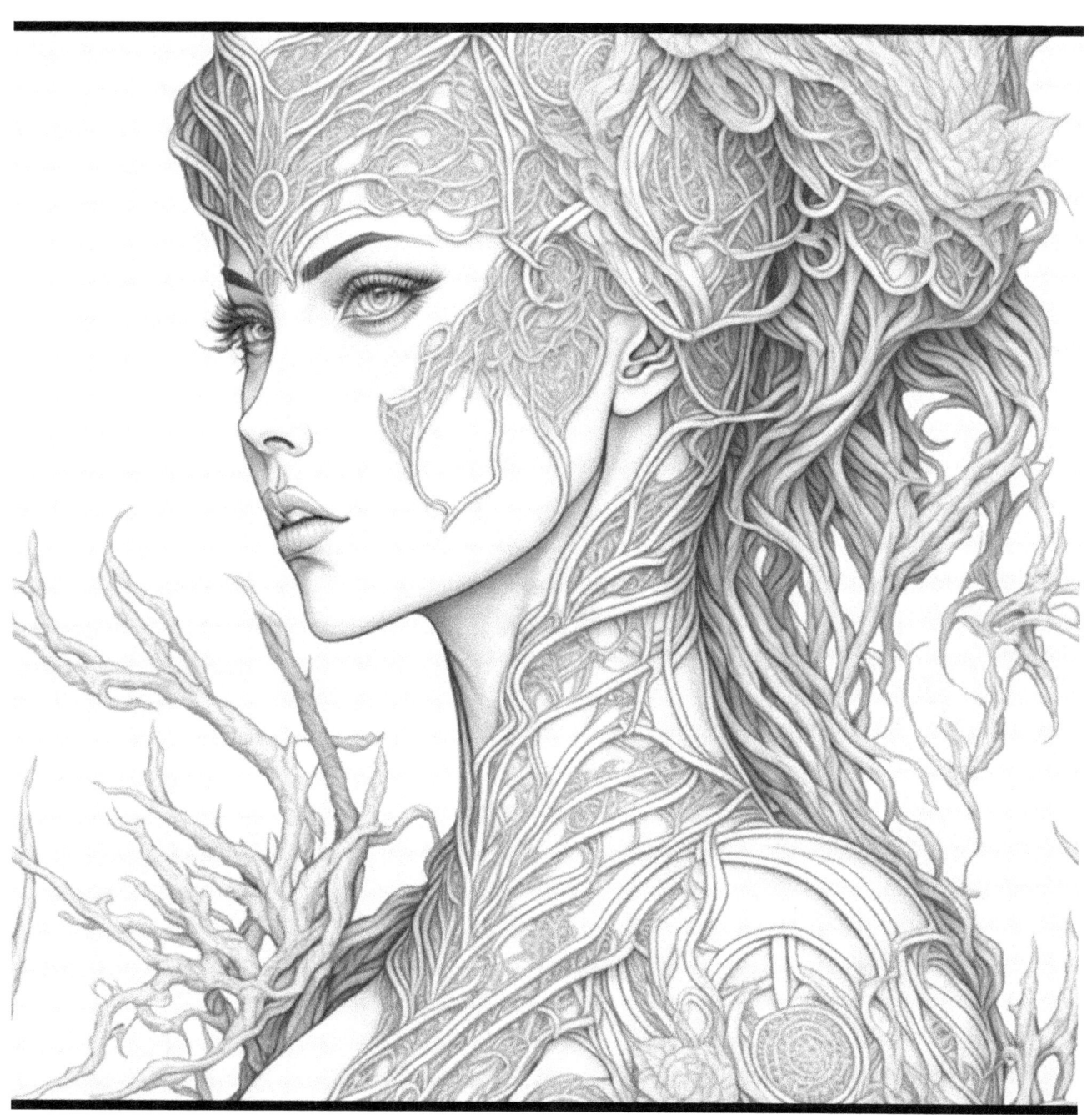

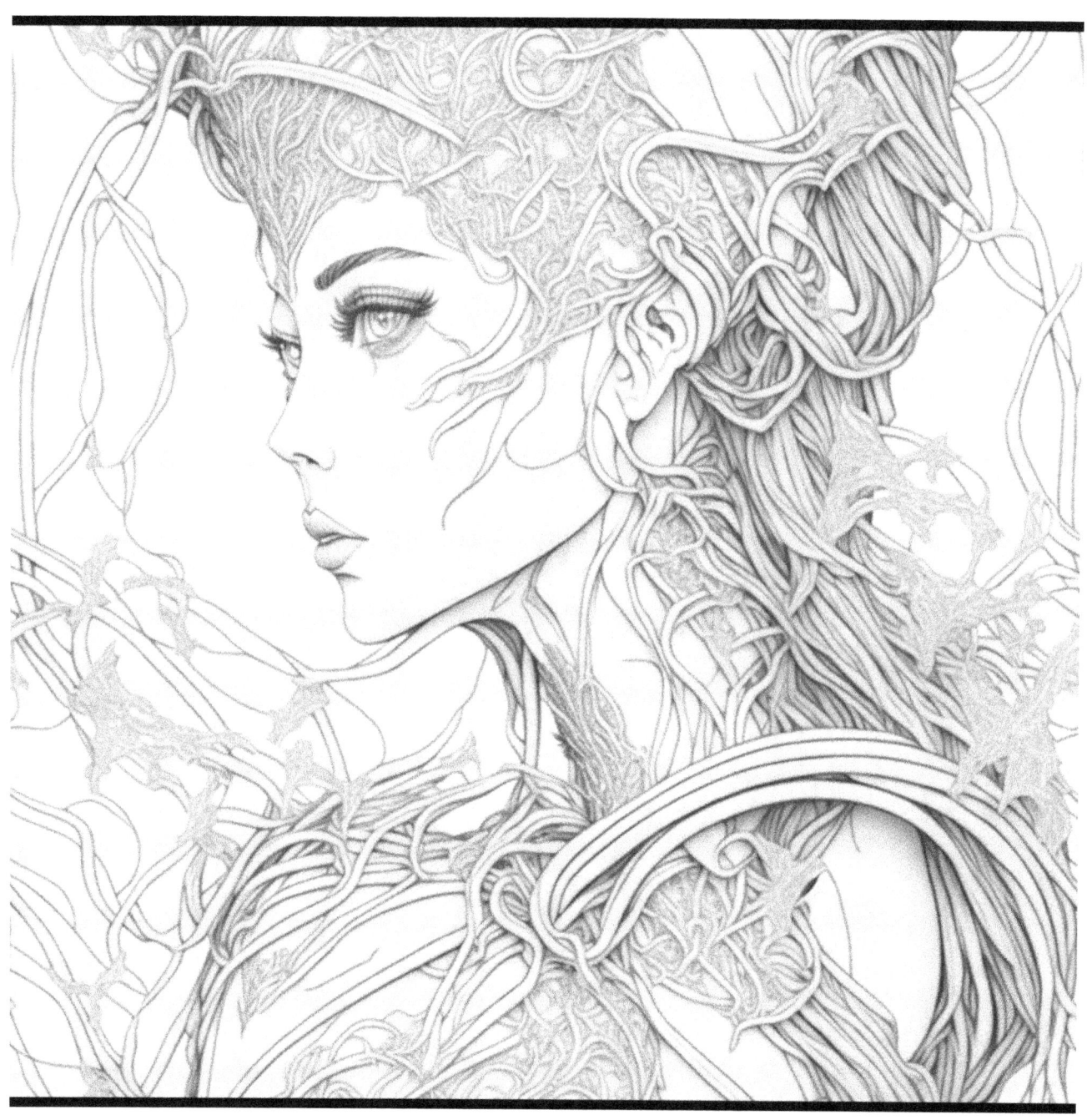

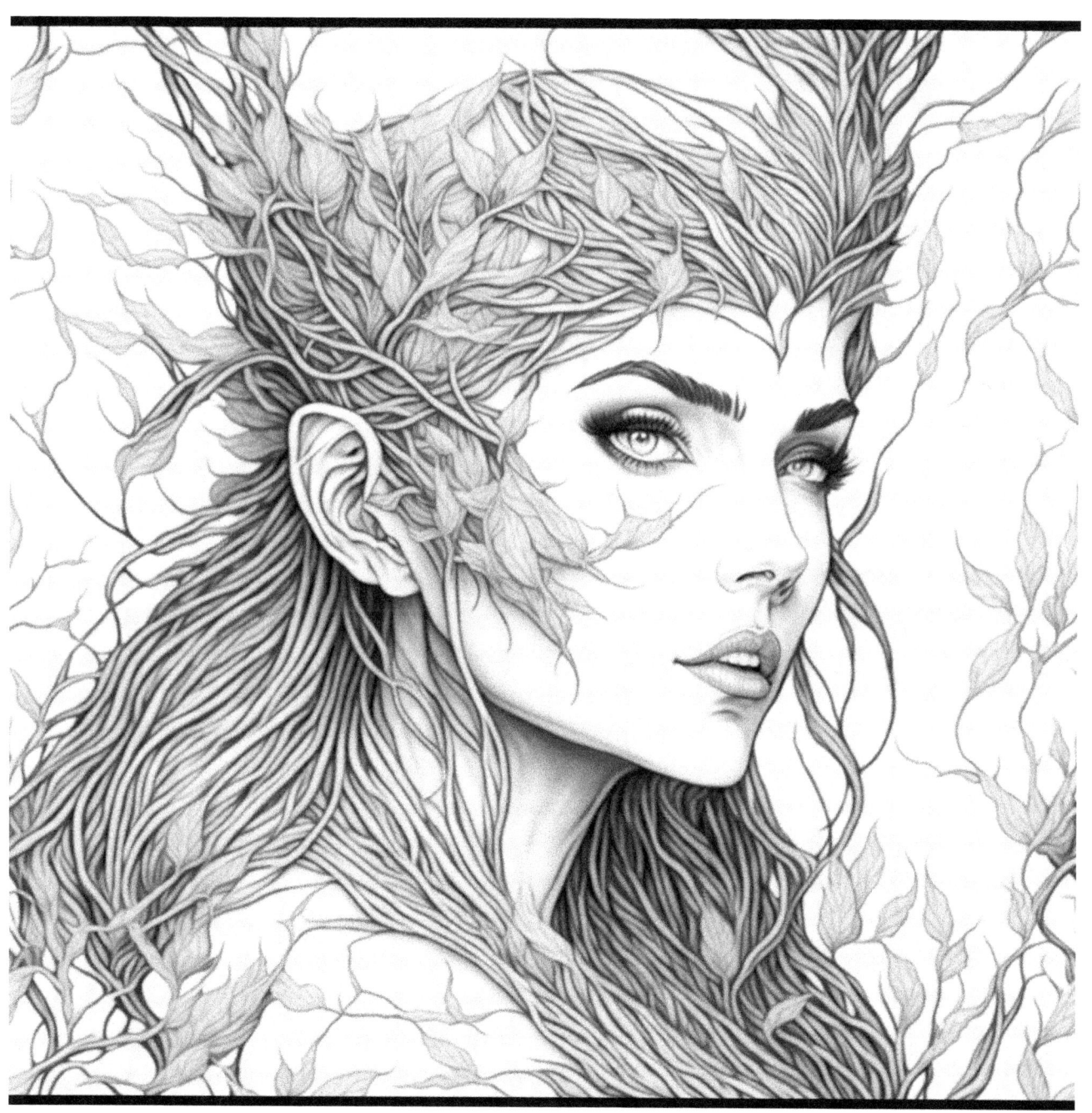

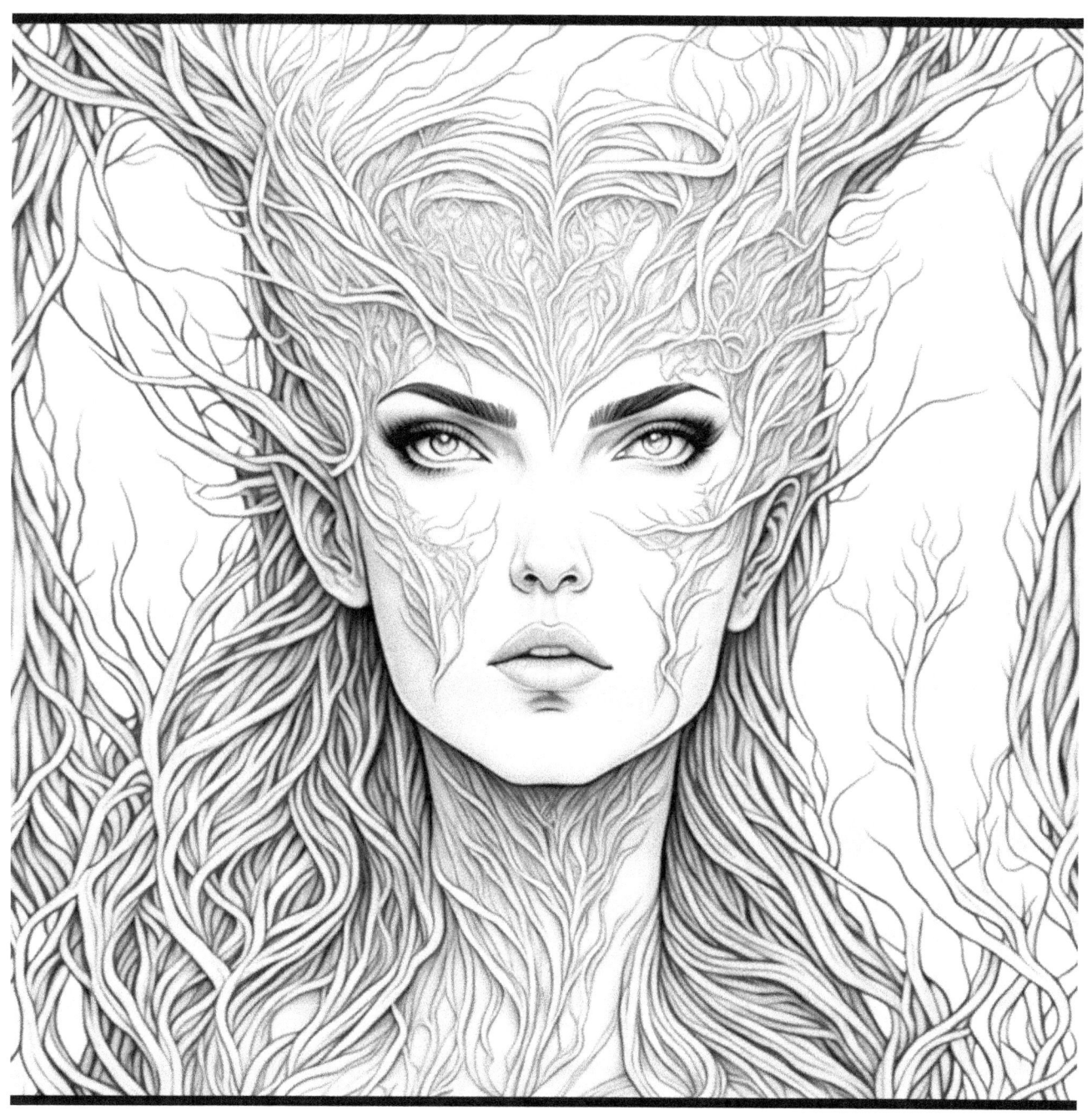

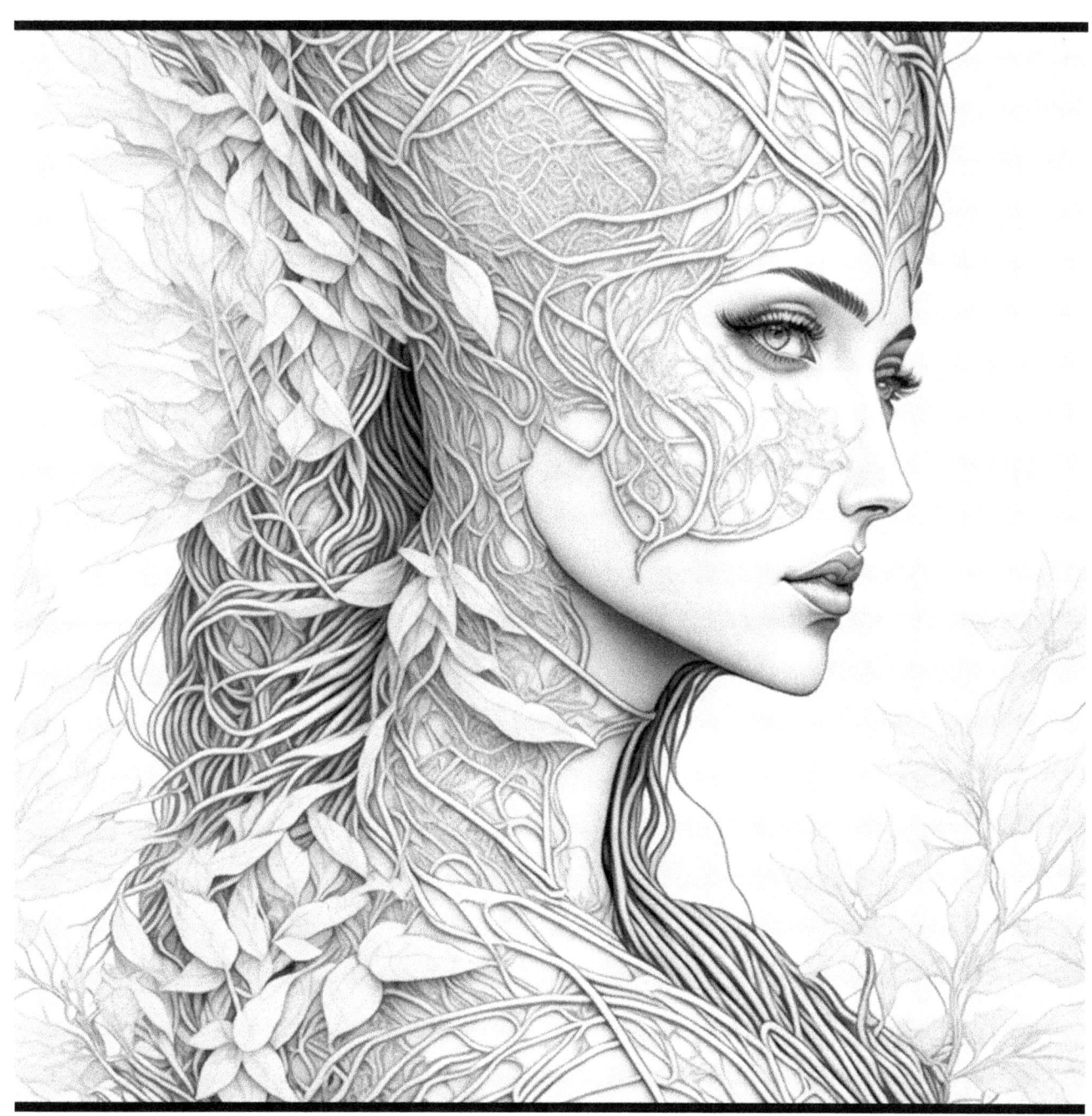

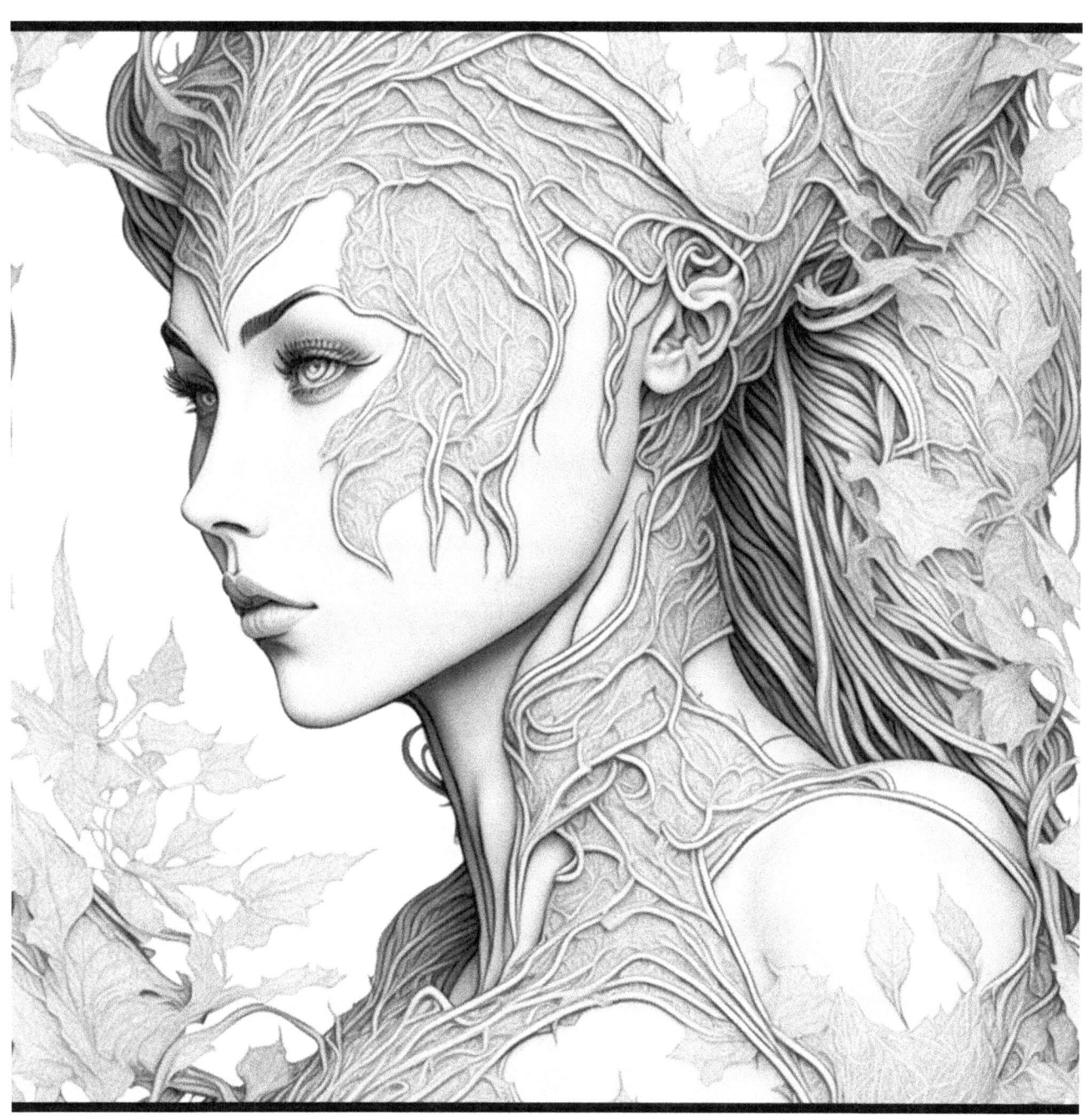

Guide Drawing

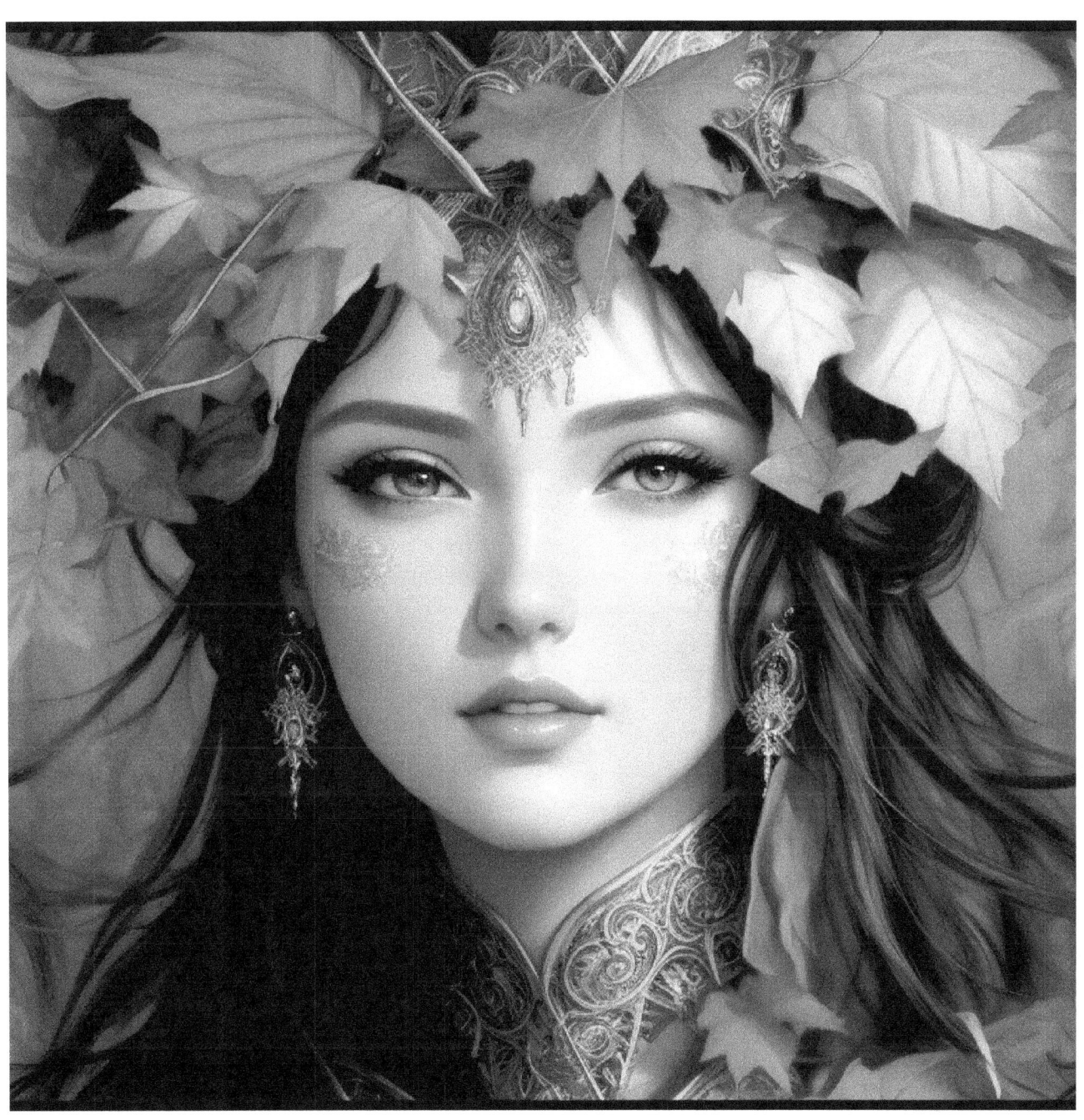

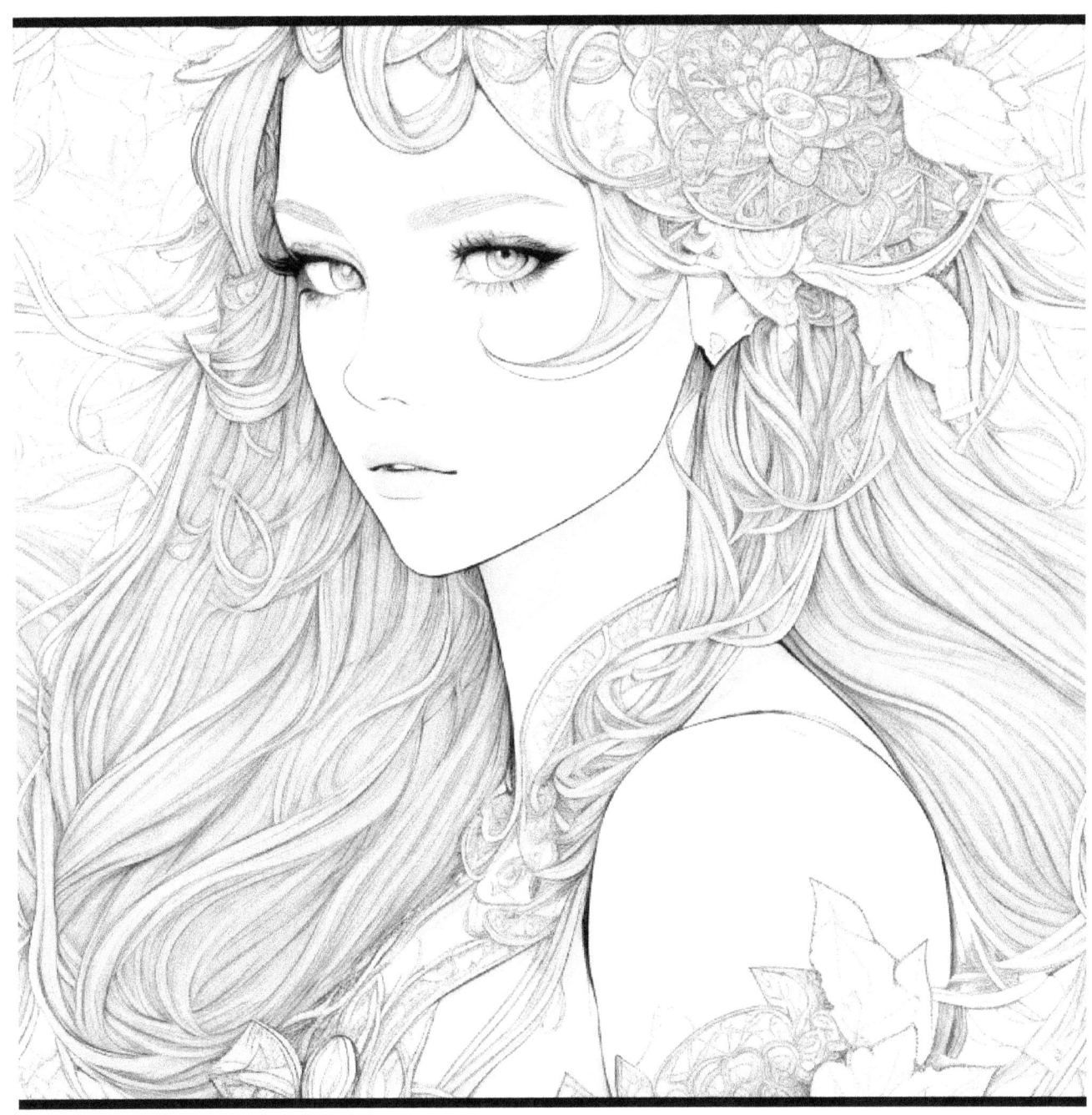

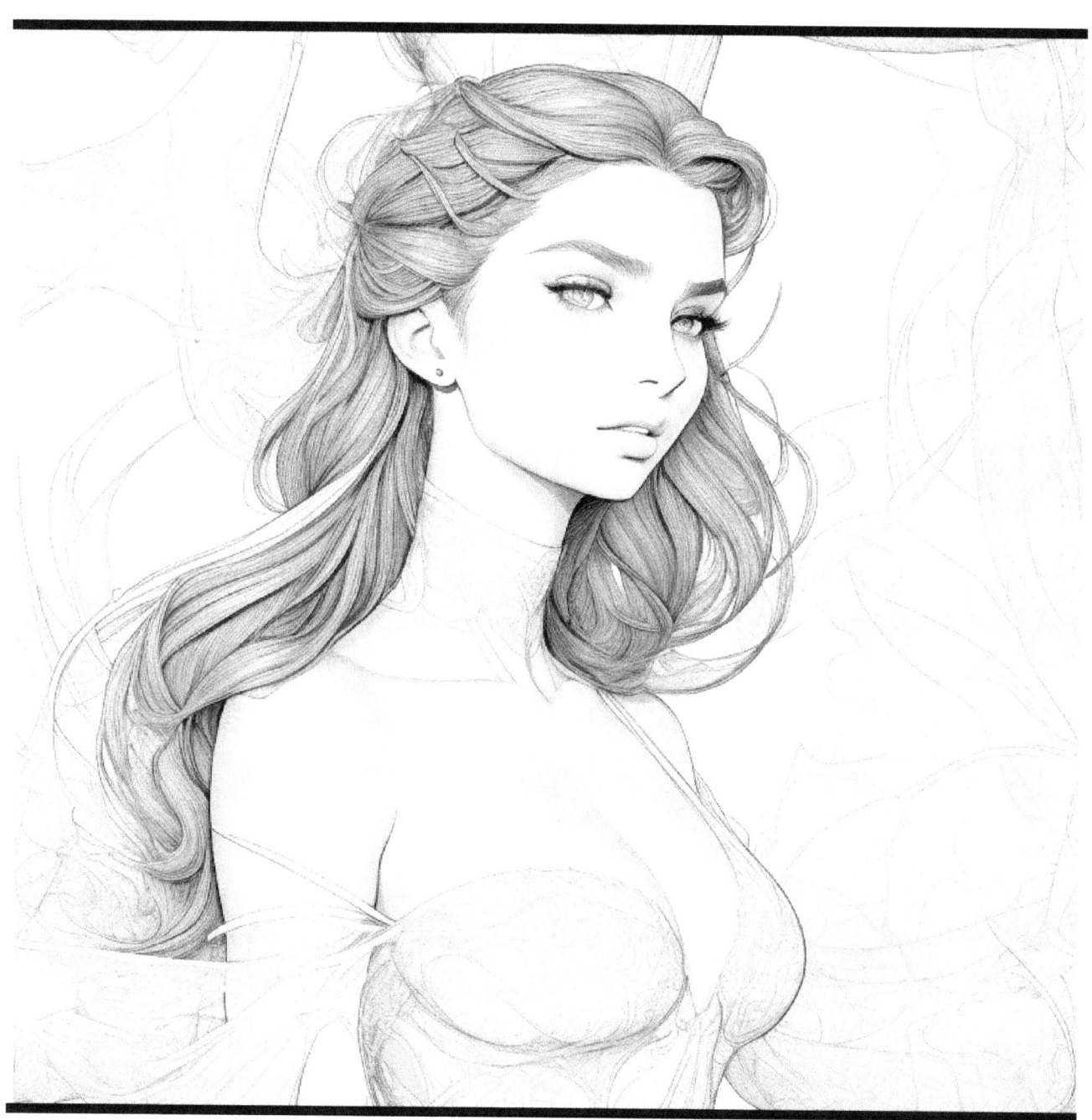

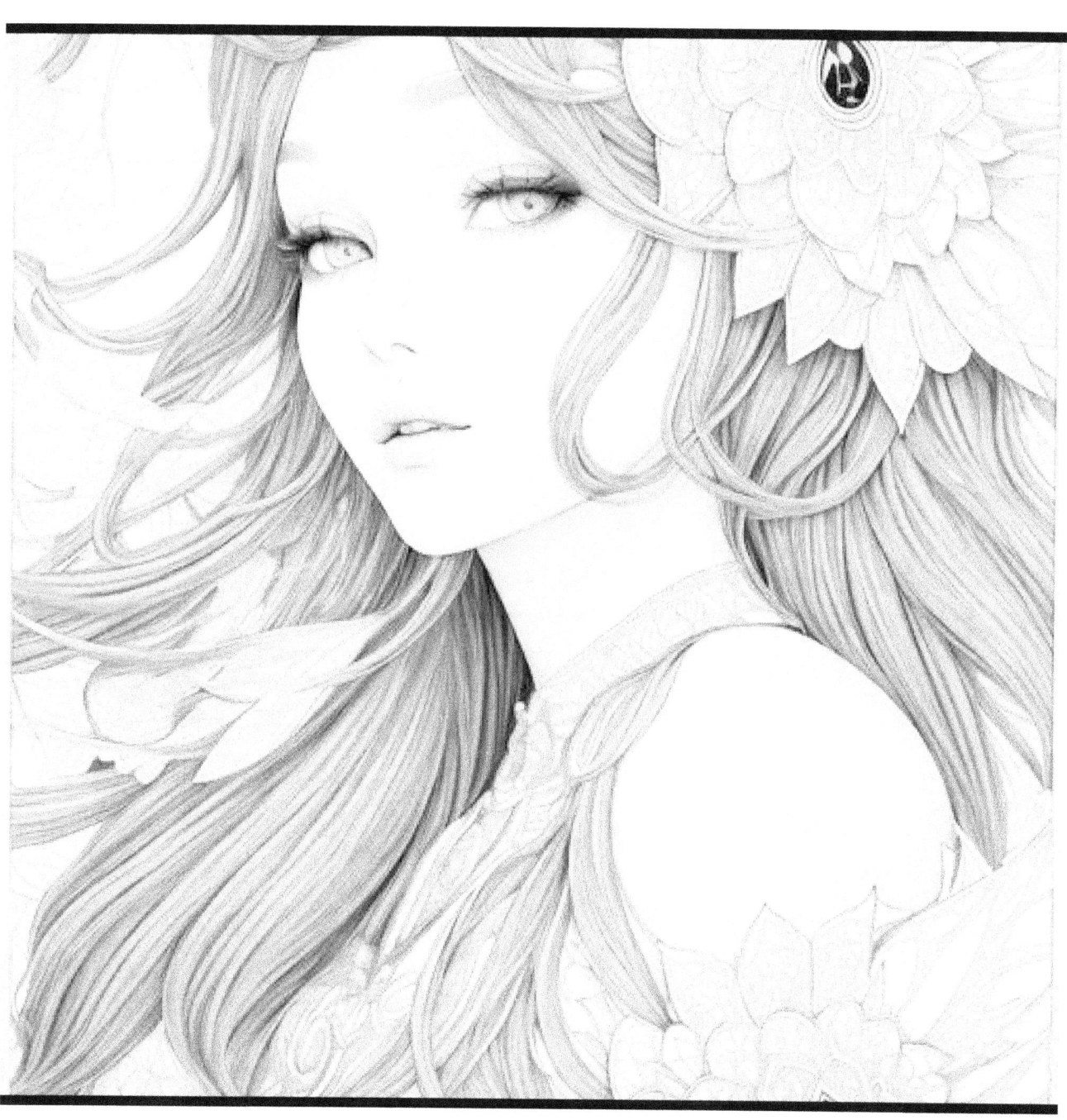

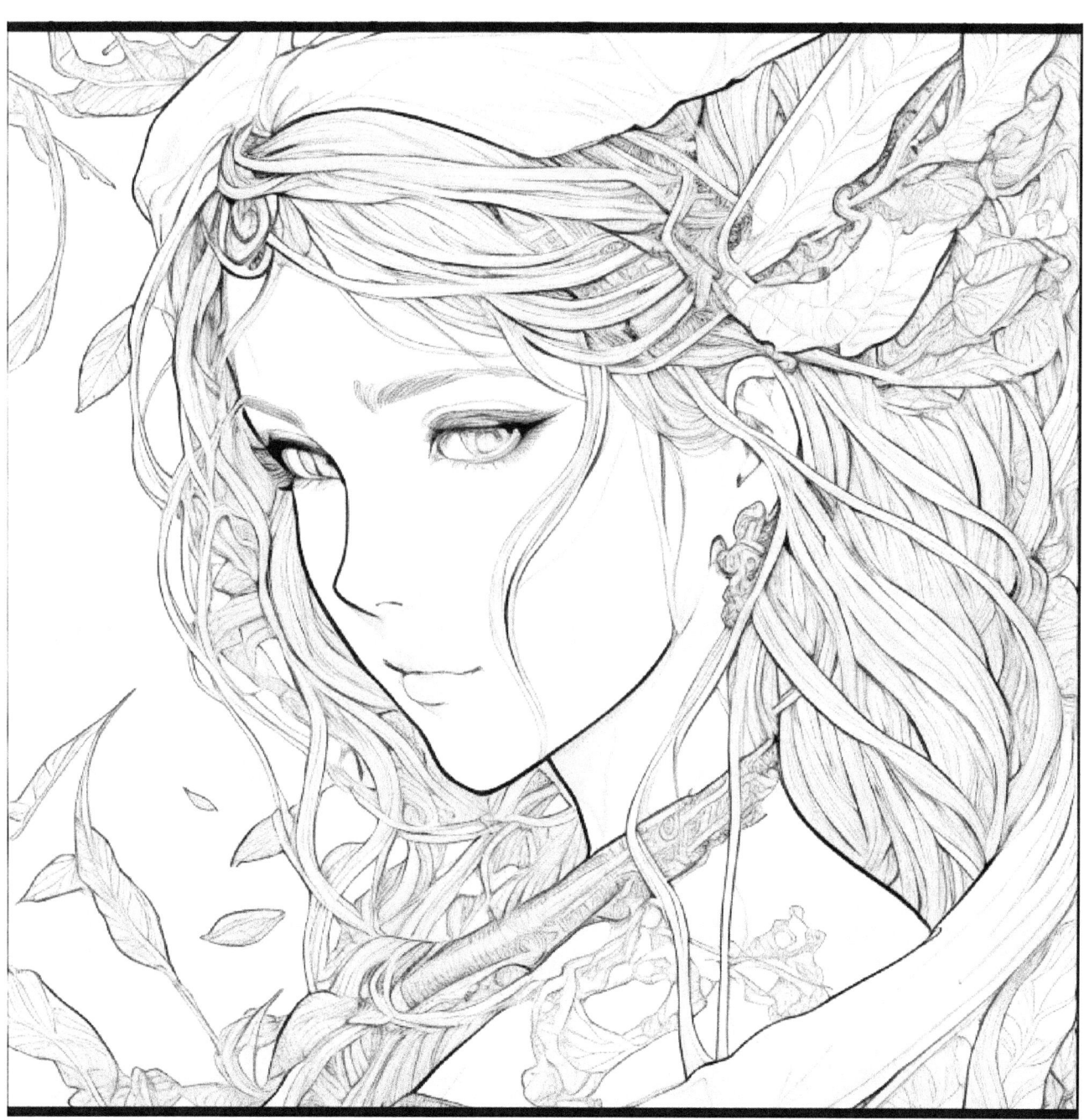

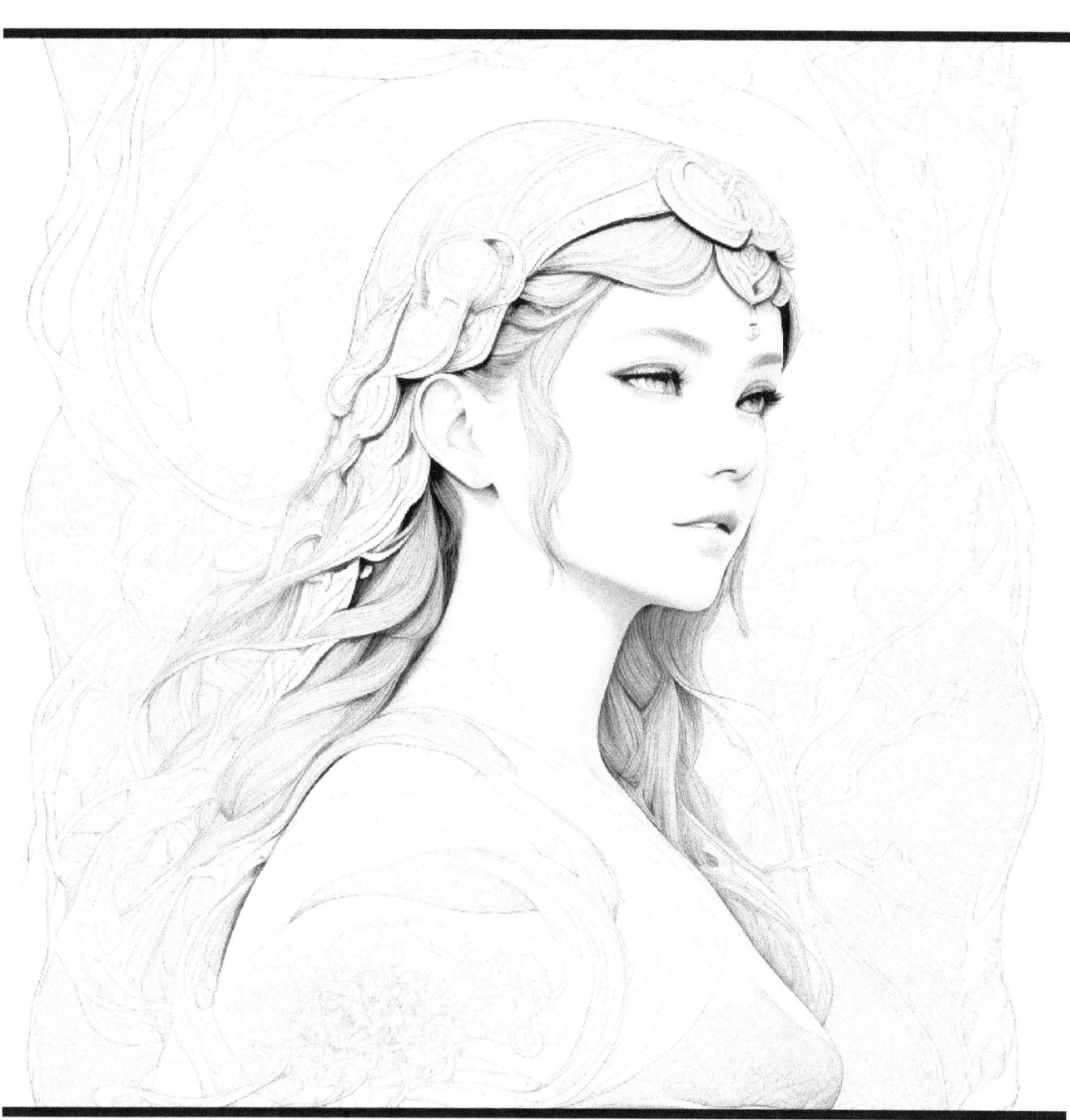

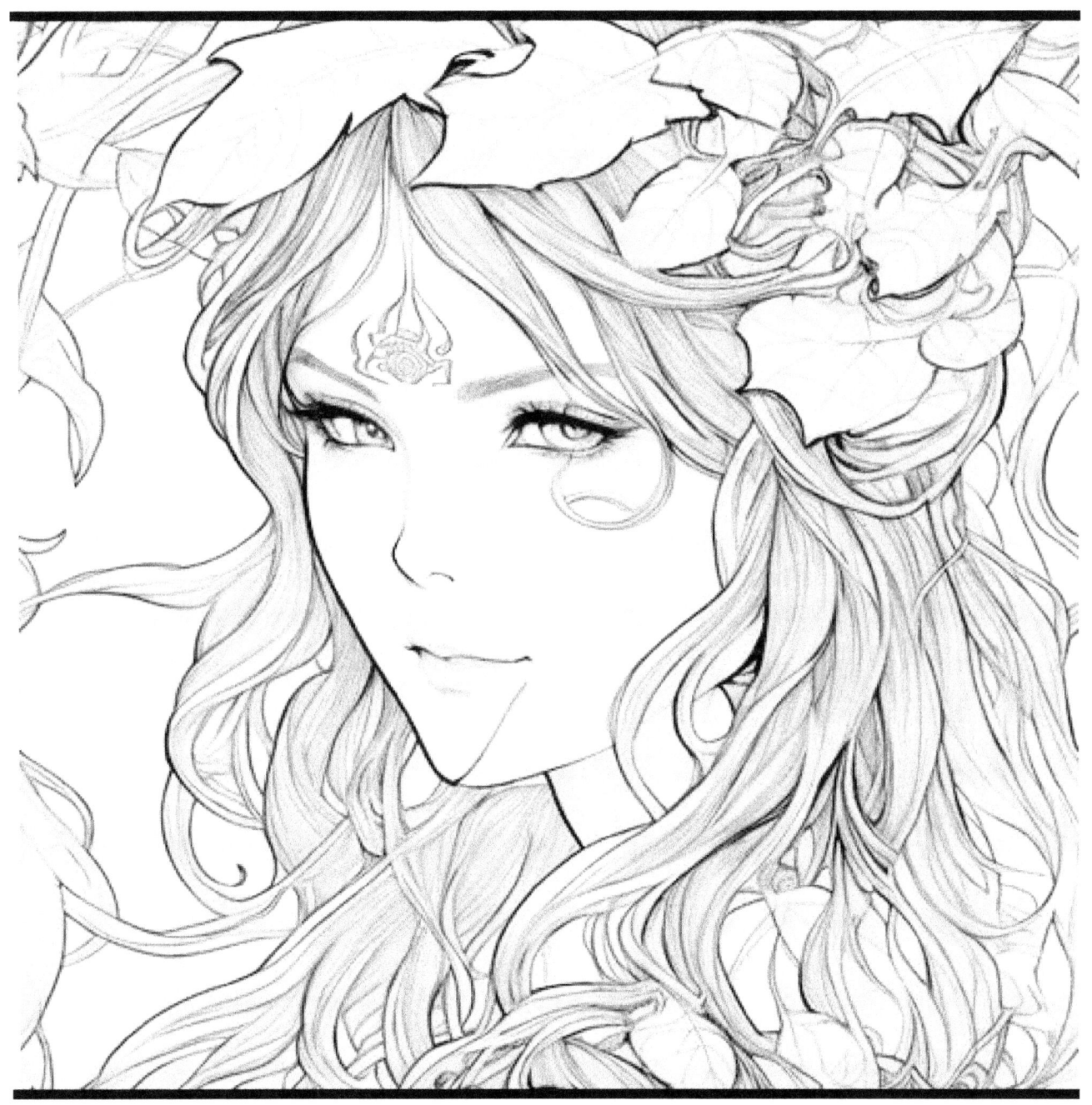

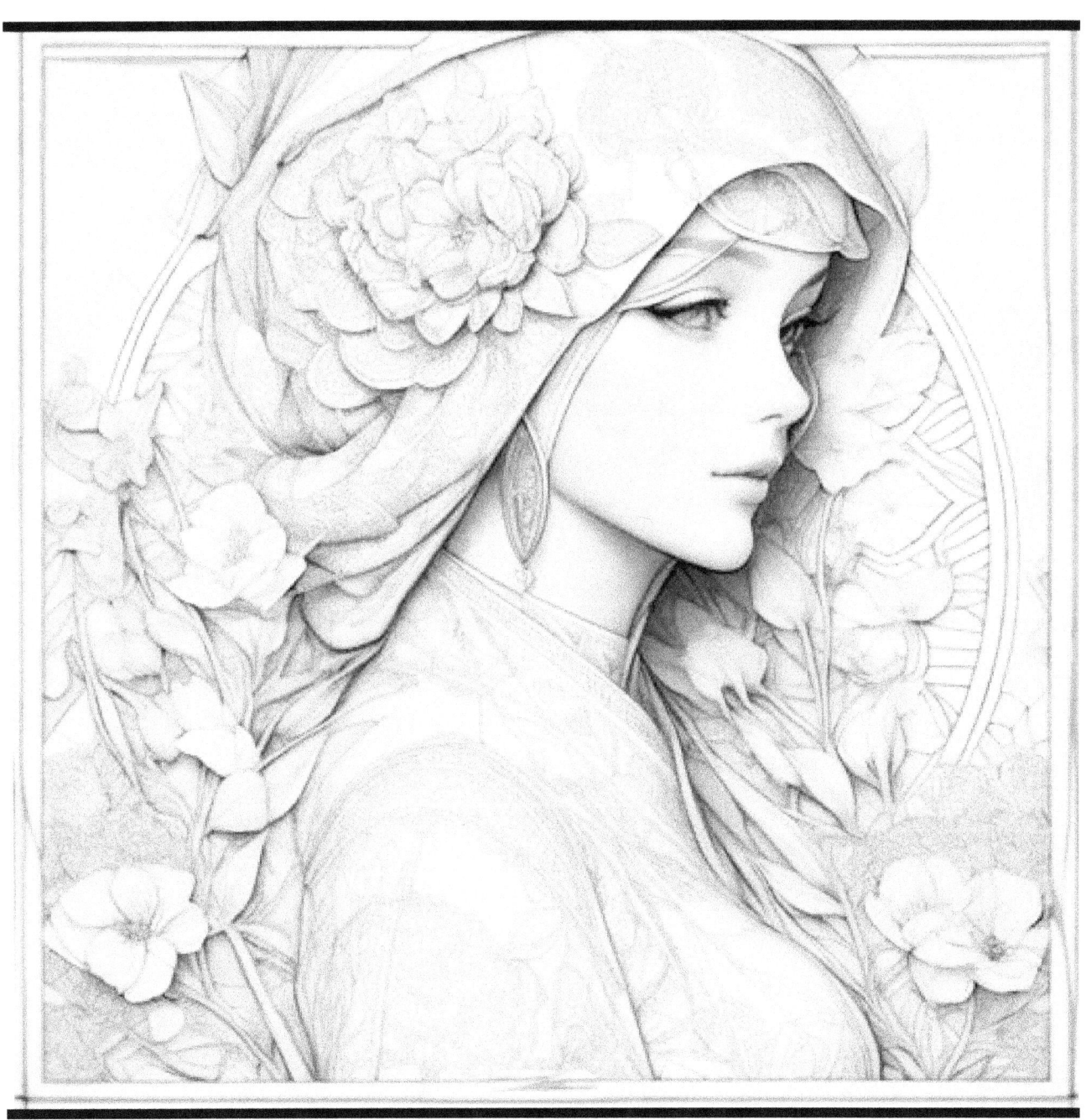

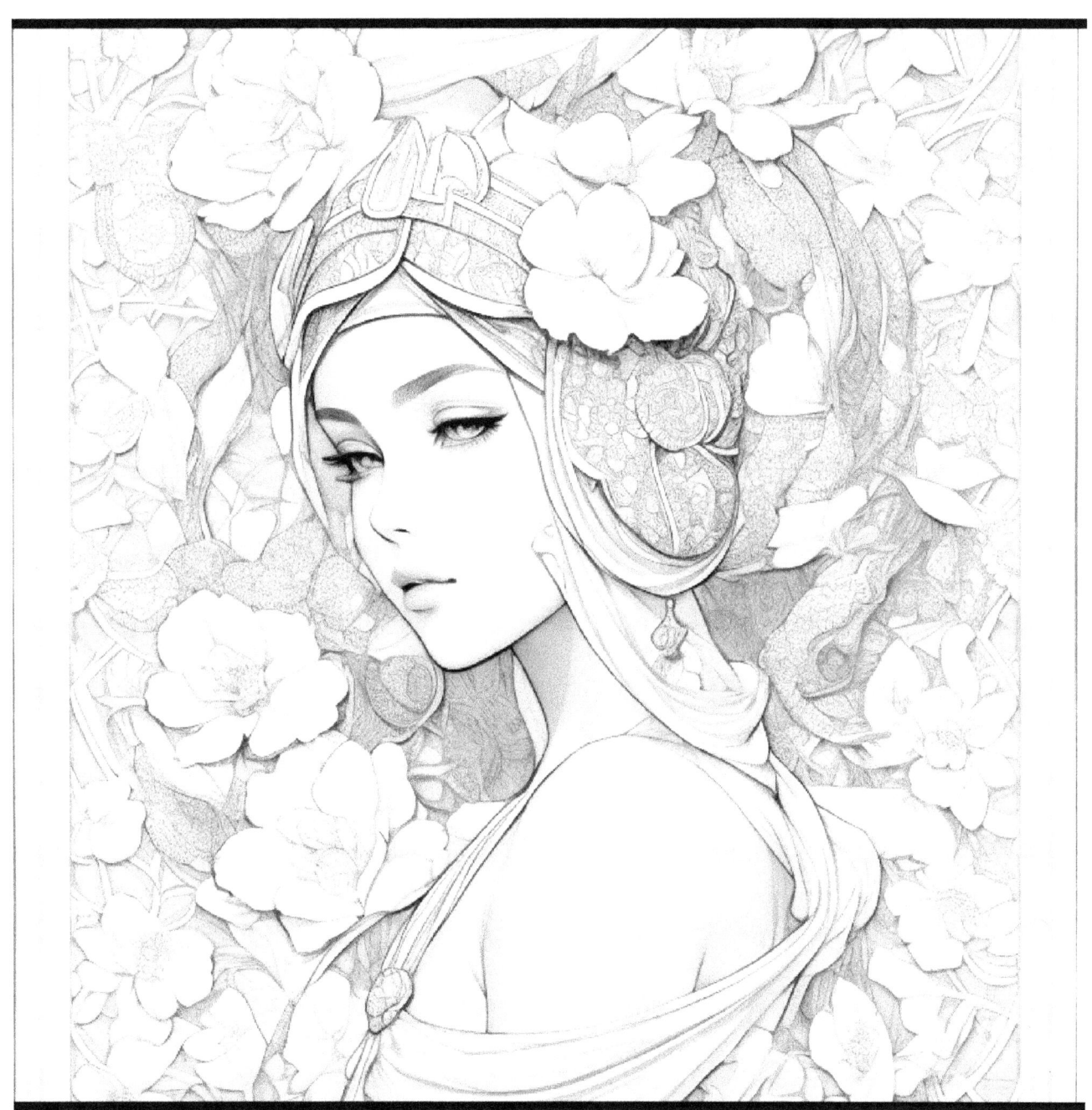

Guide Drawing

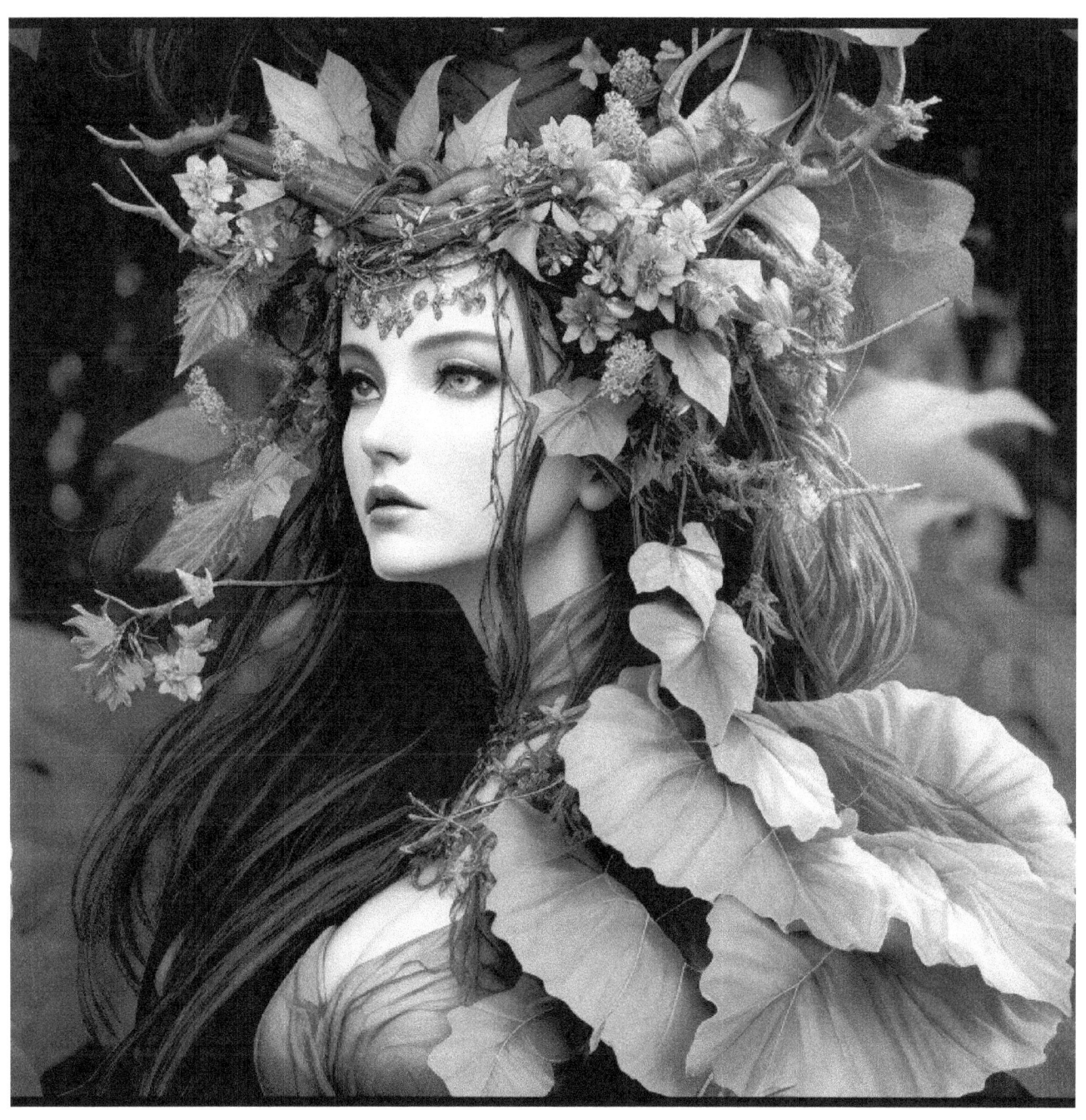

Guide Drawing

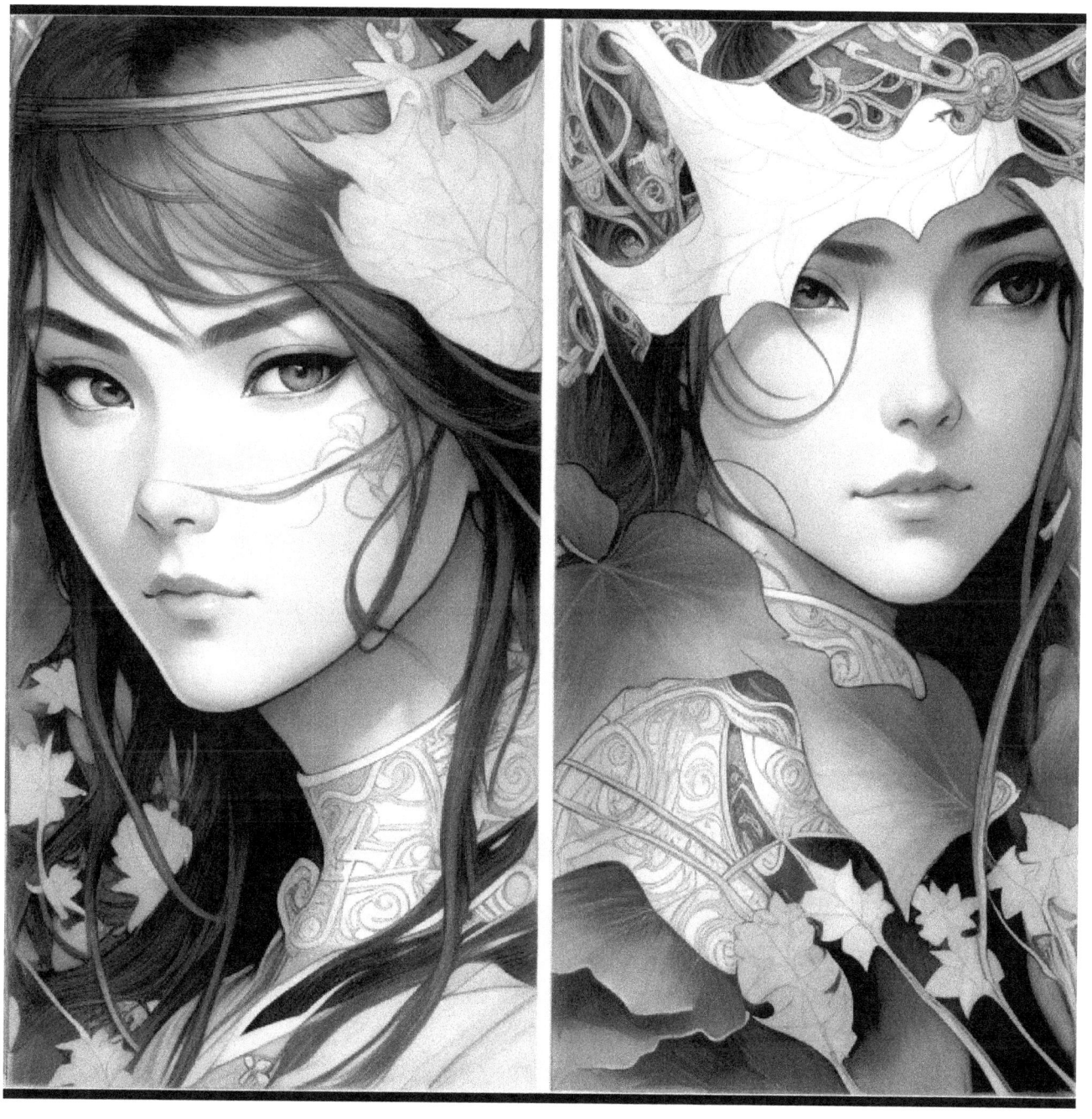

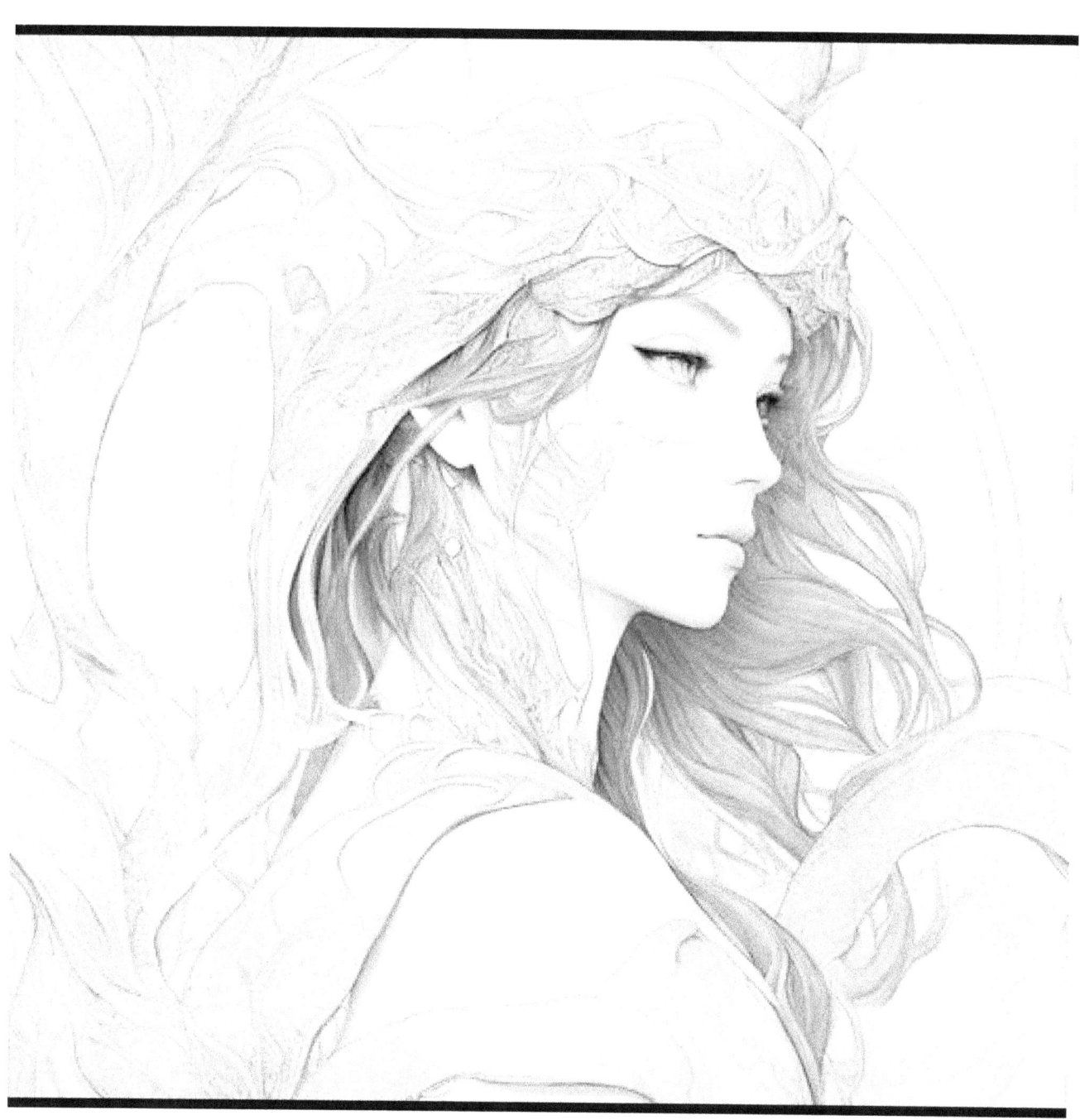

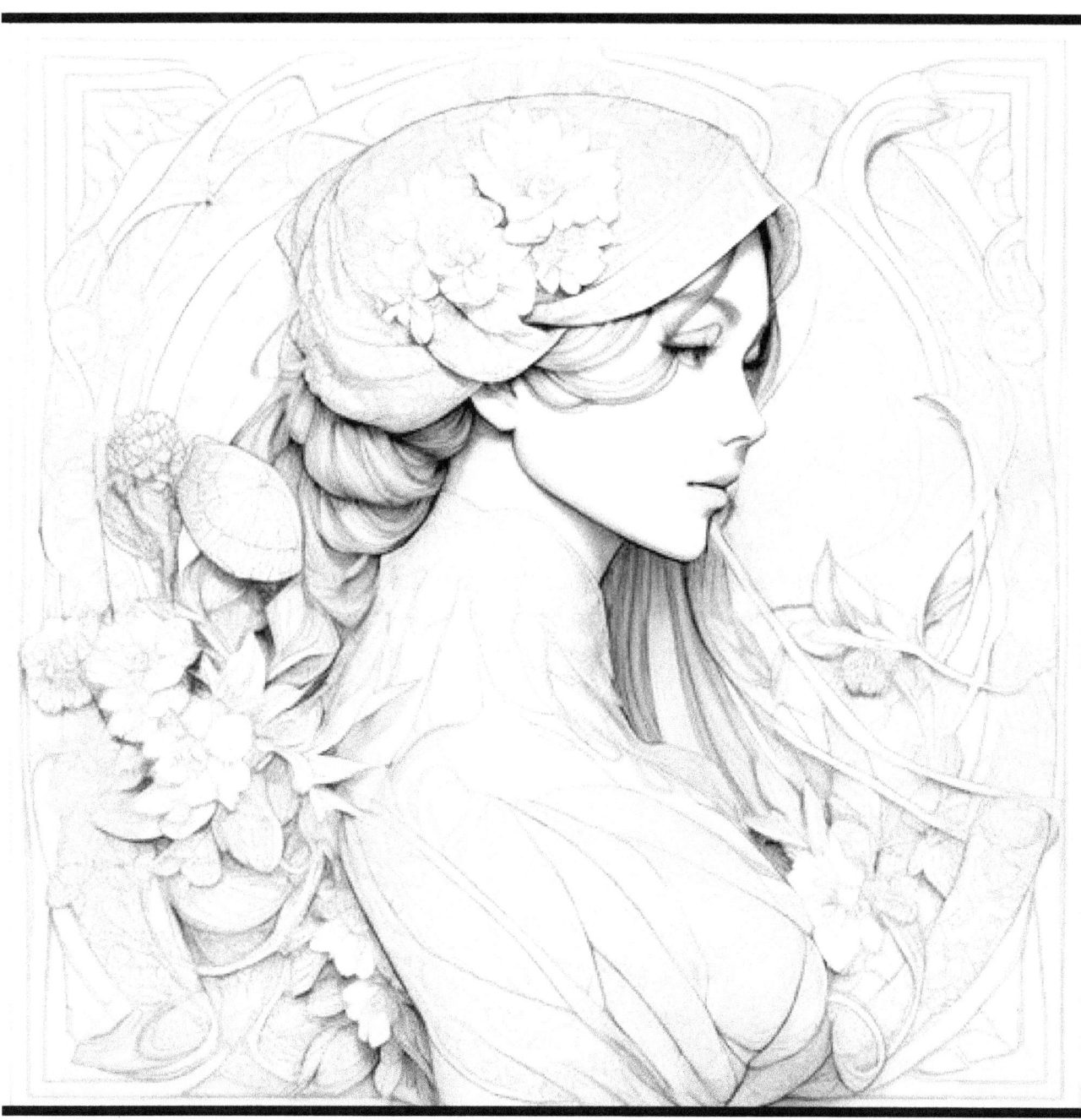

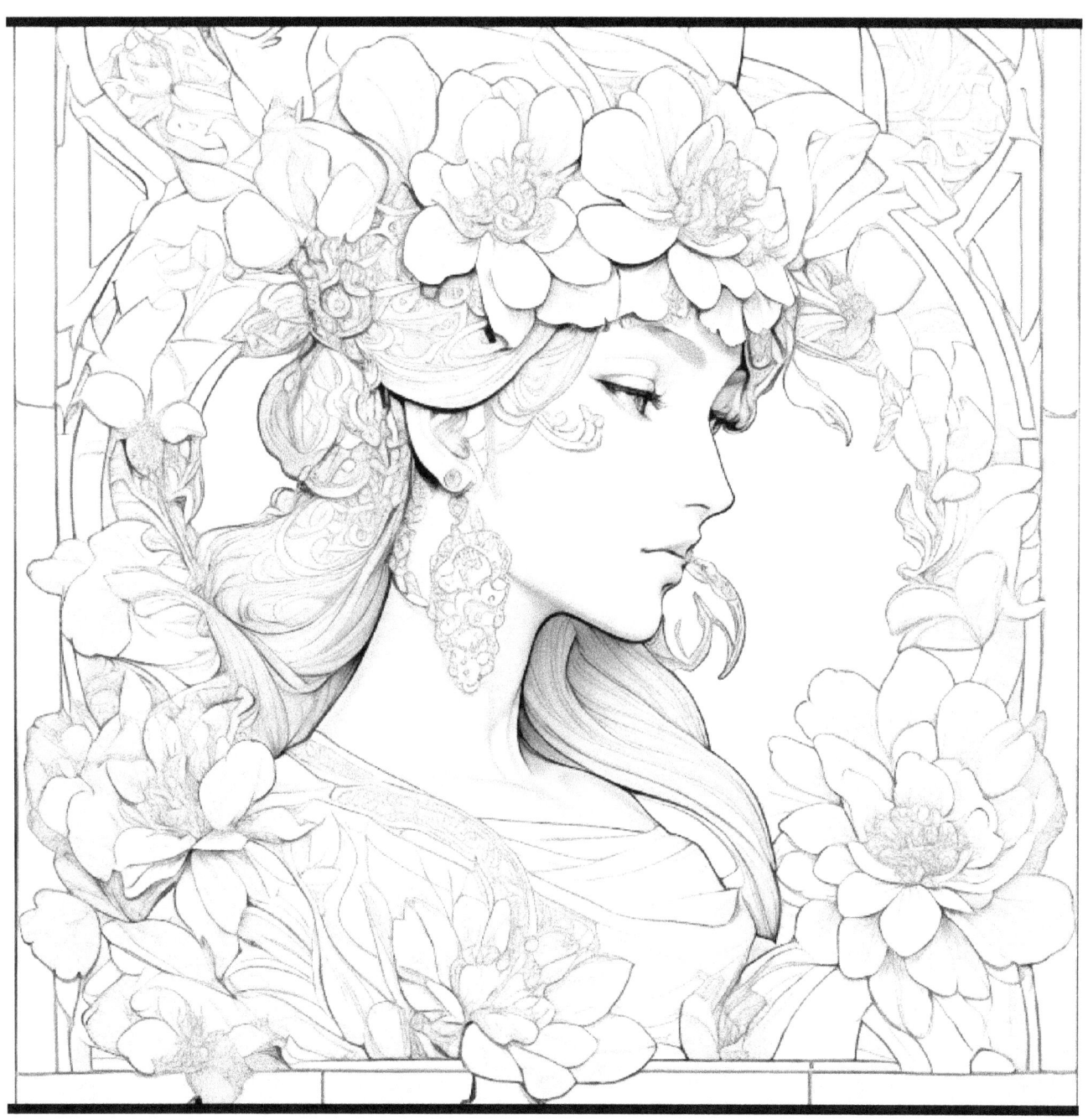

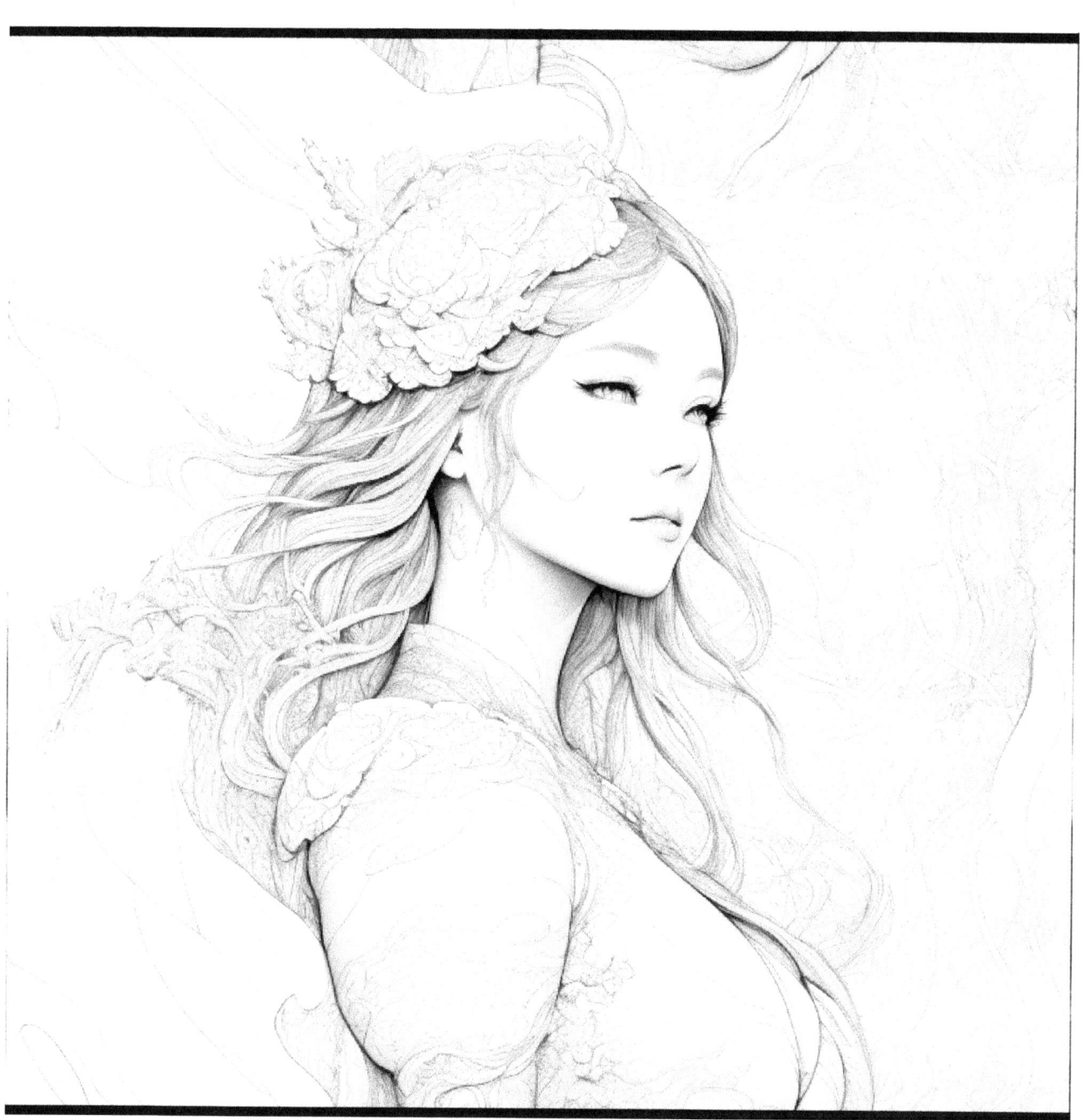

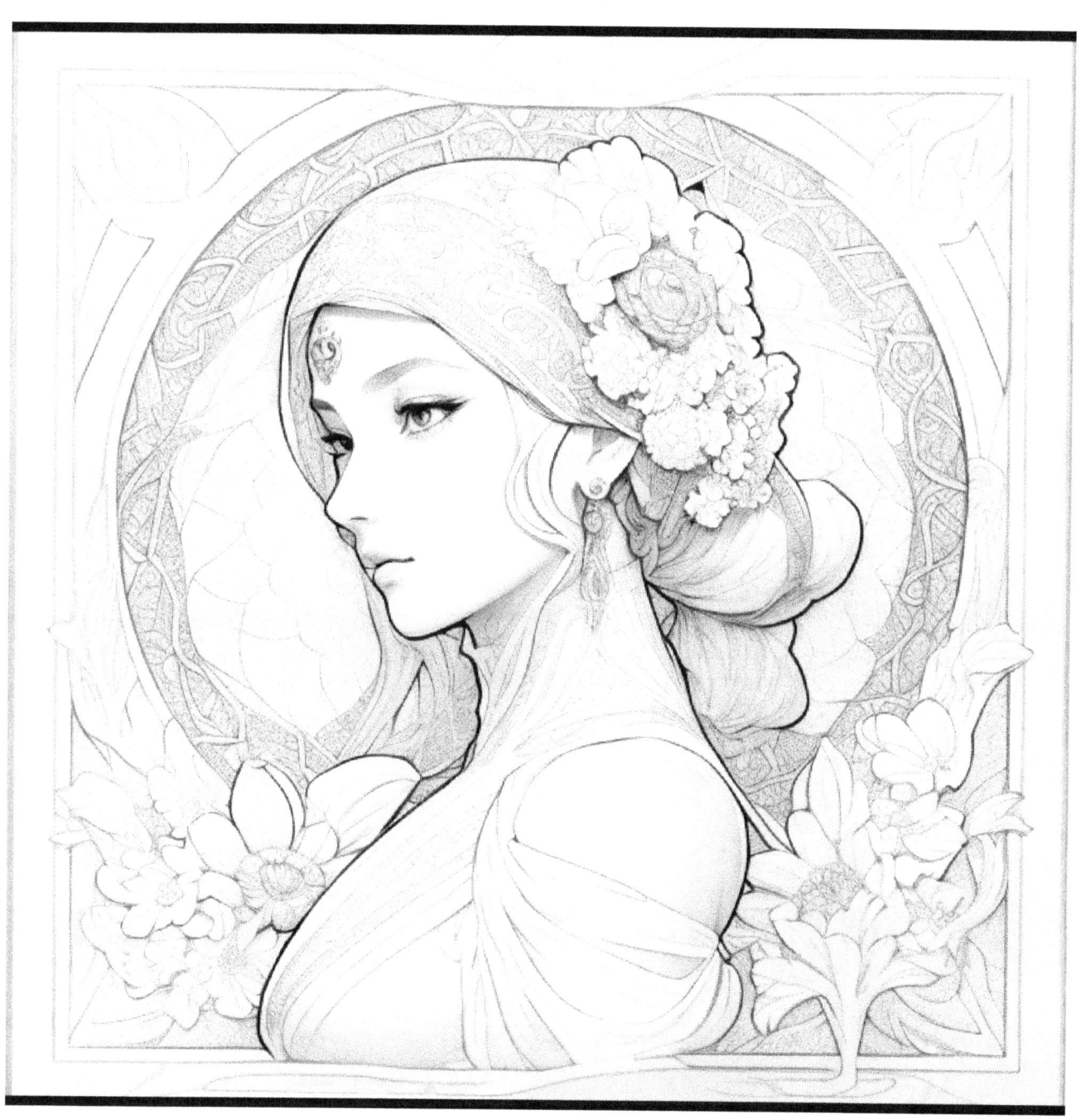

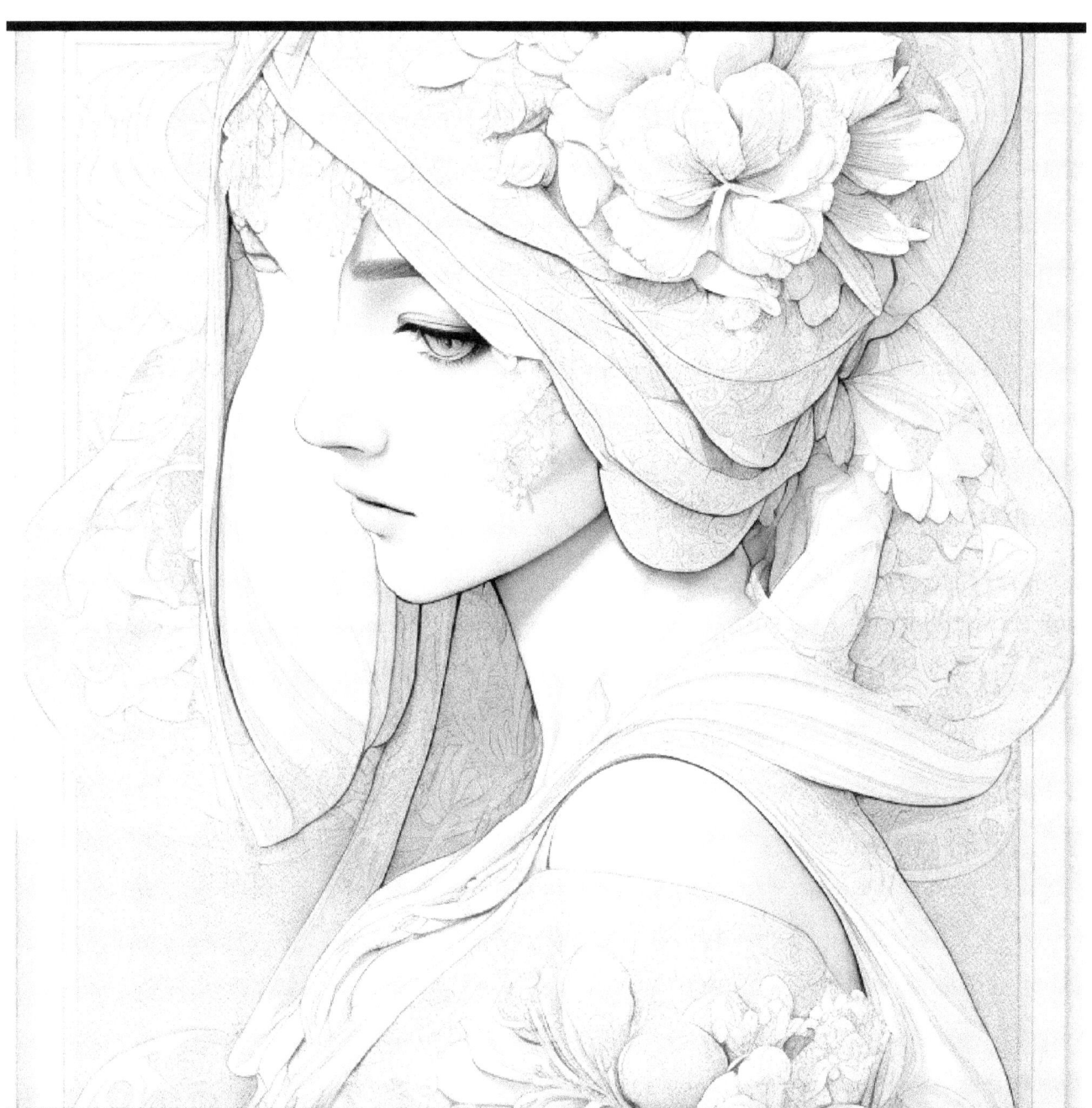

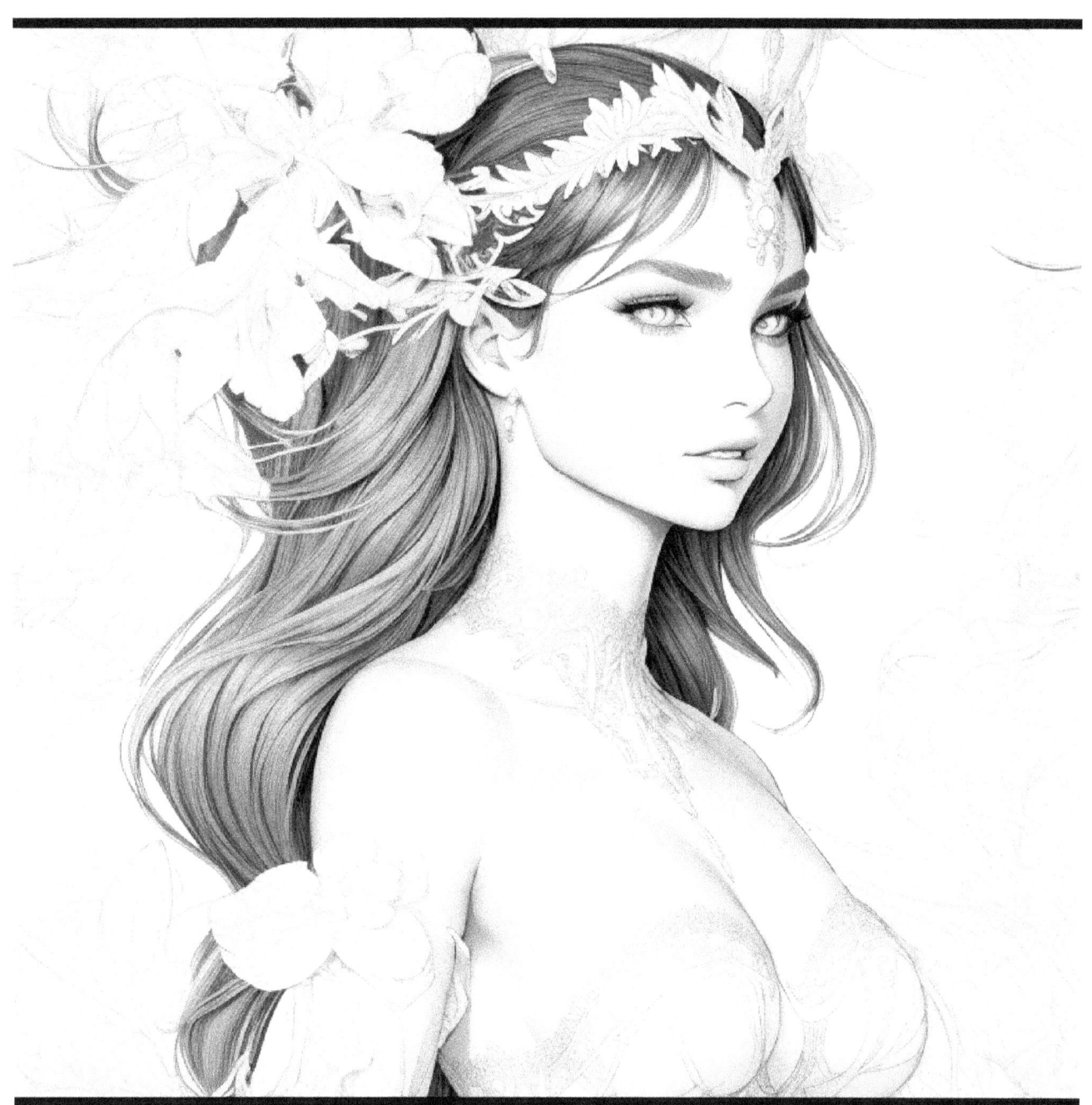

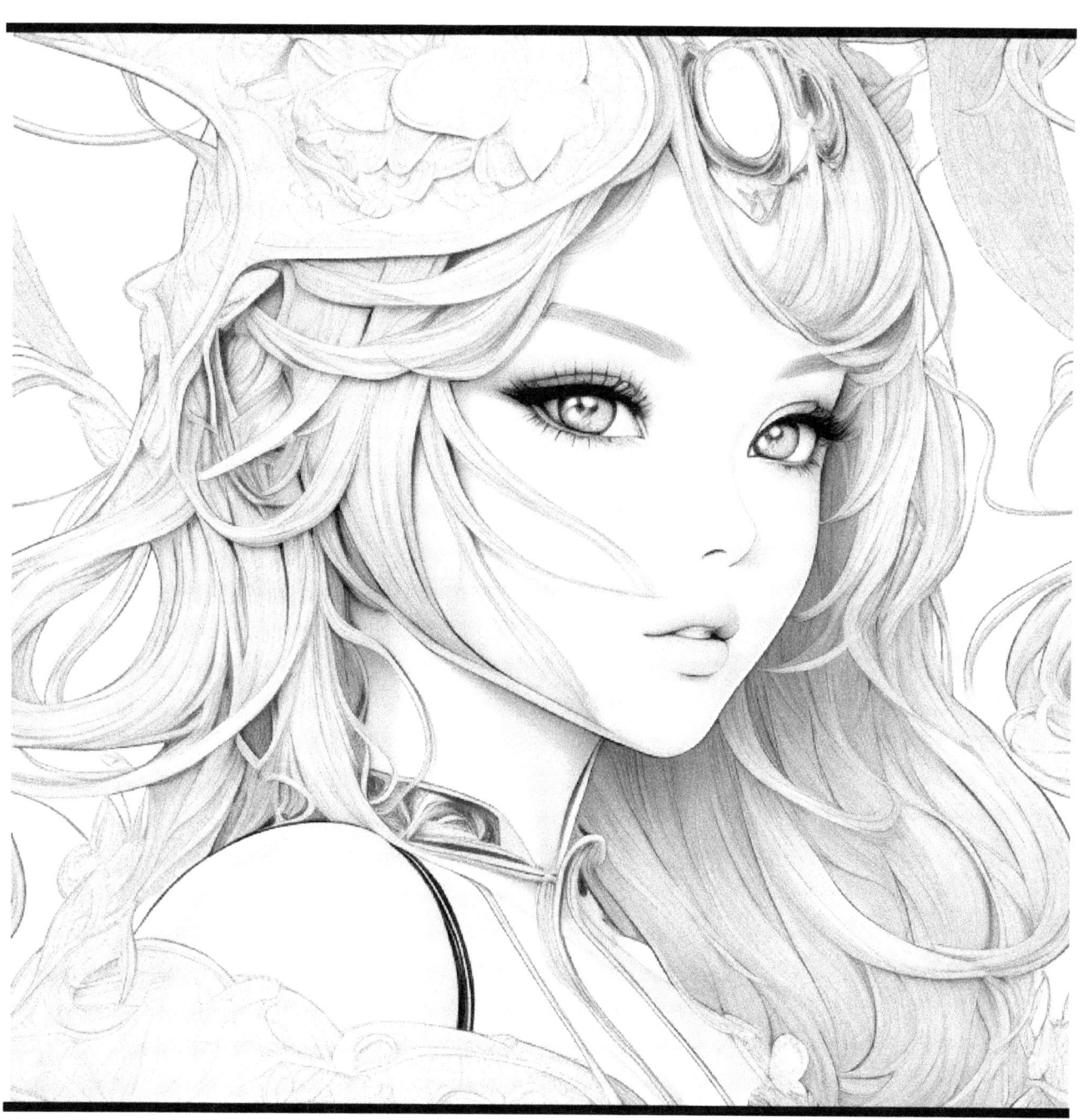

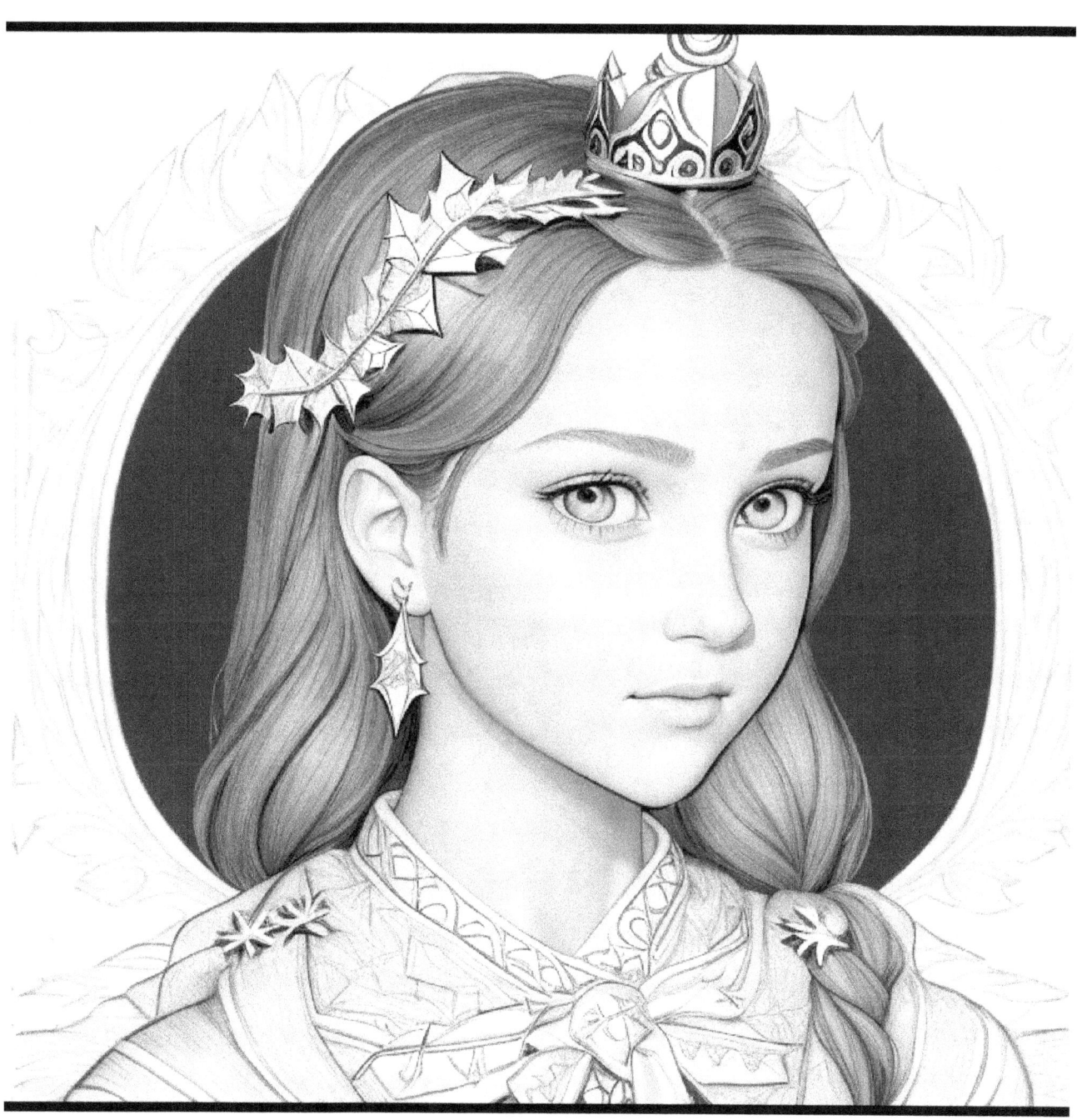

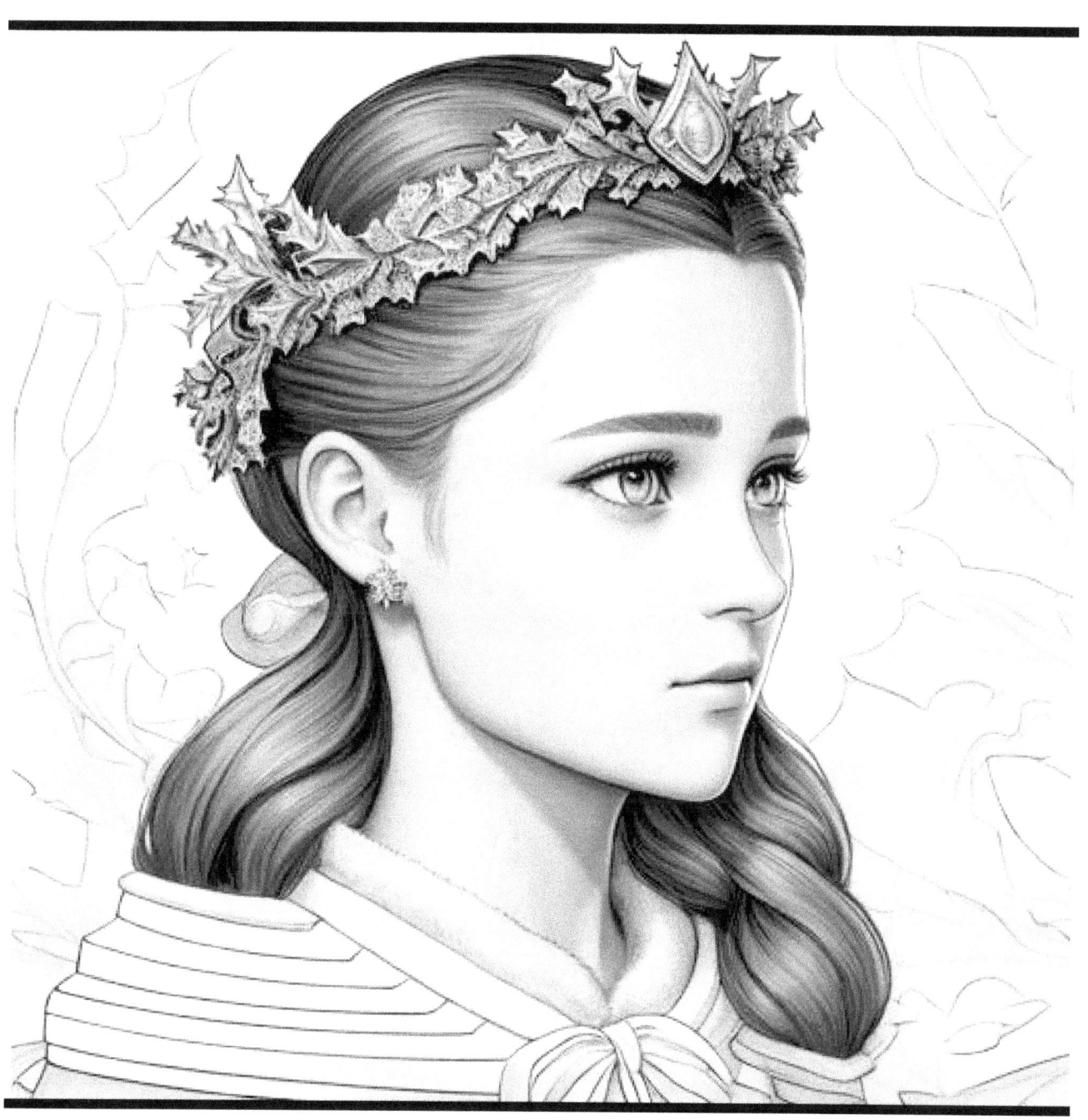

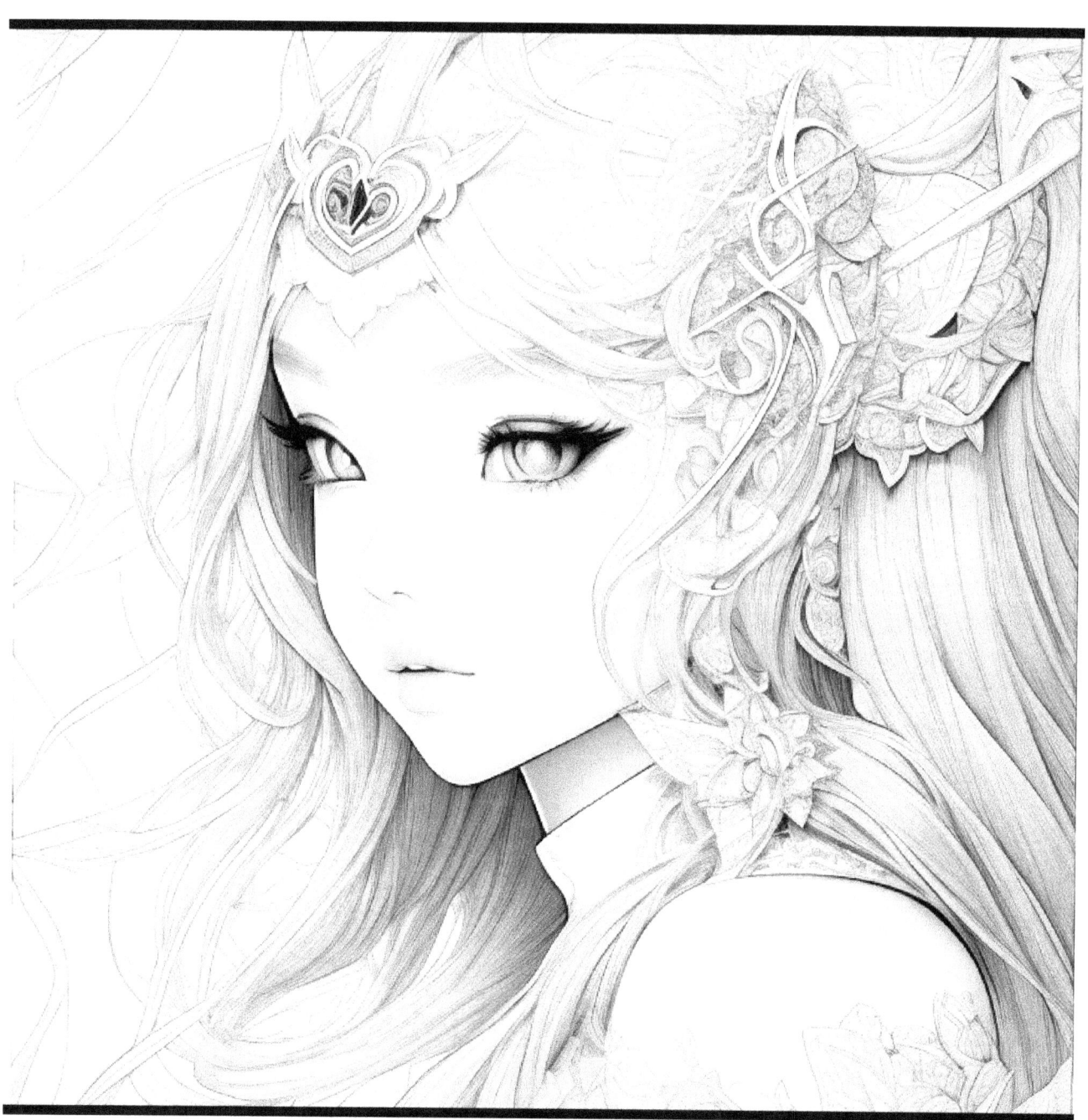

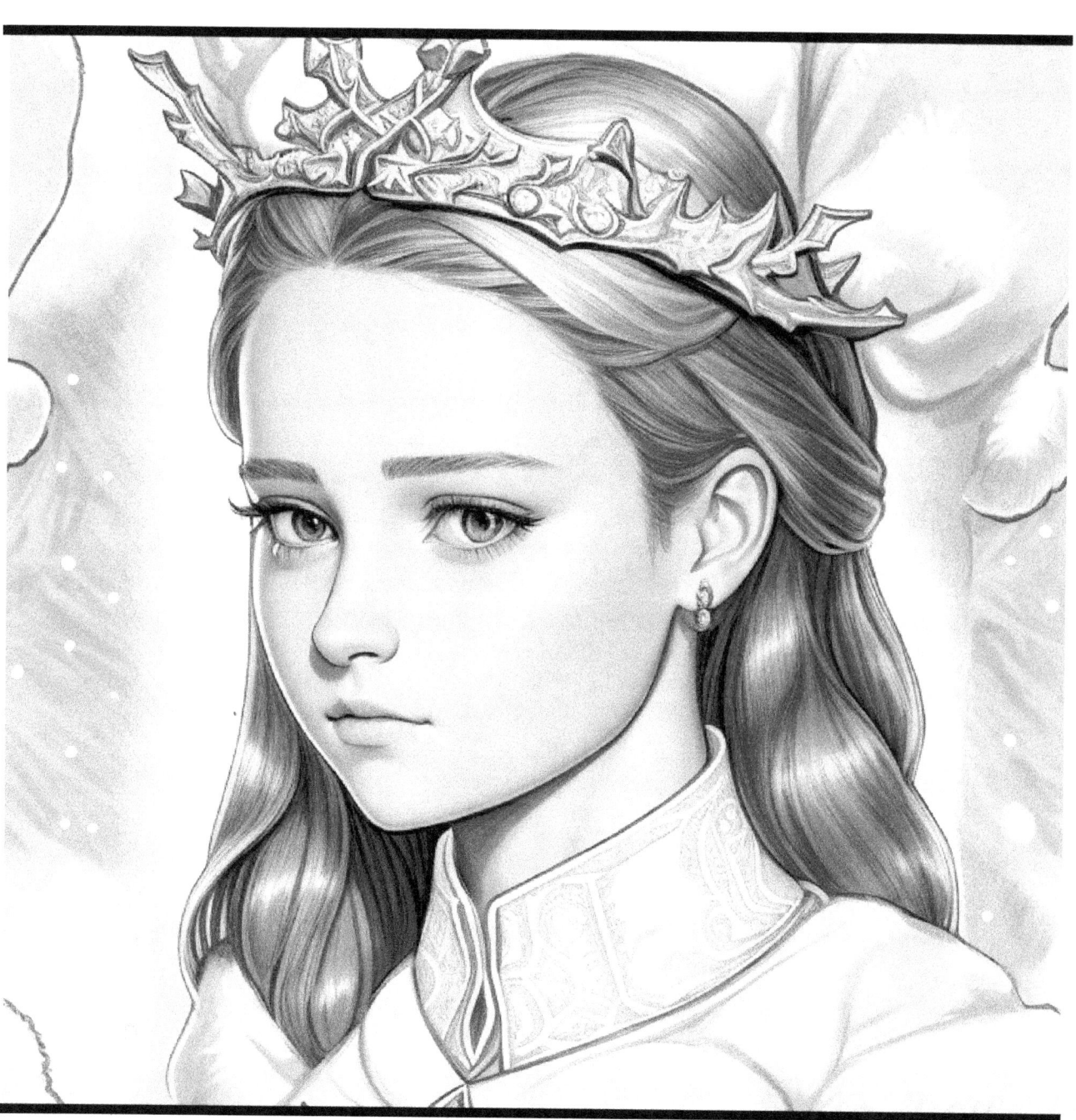

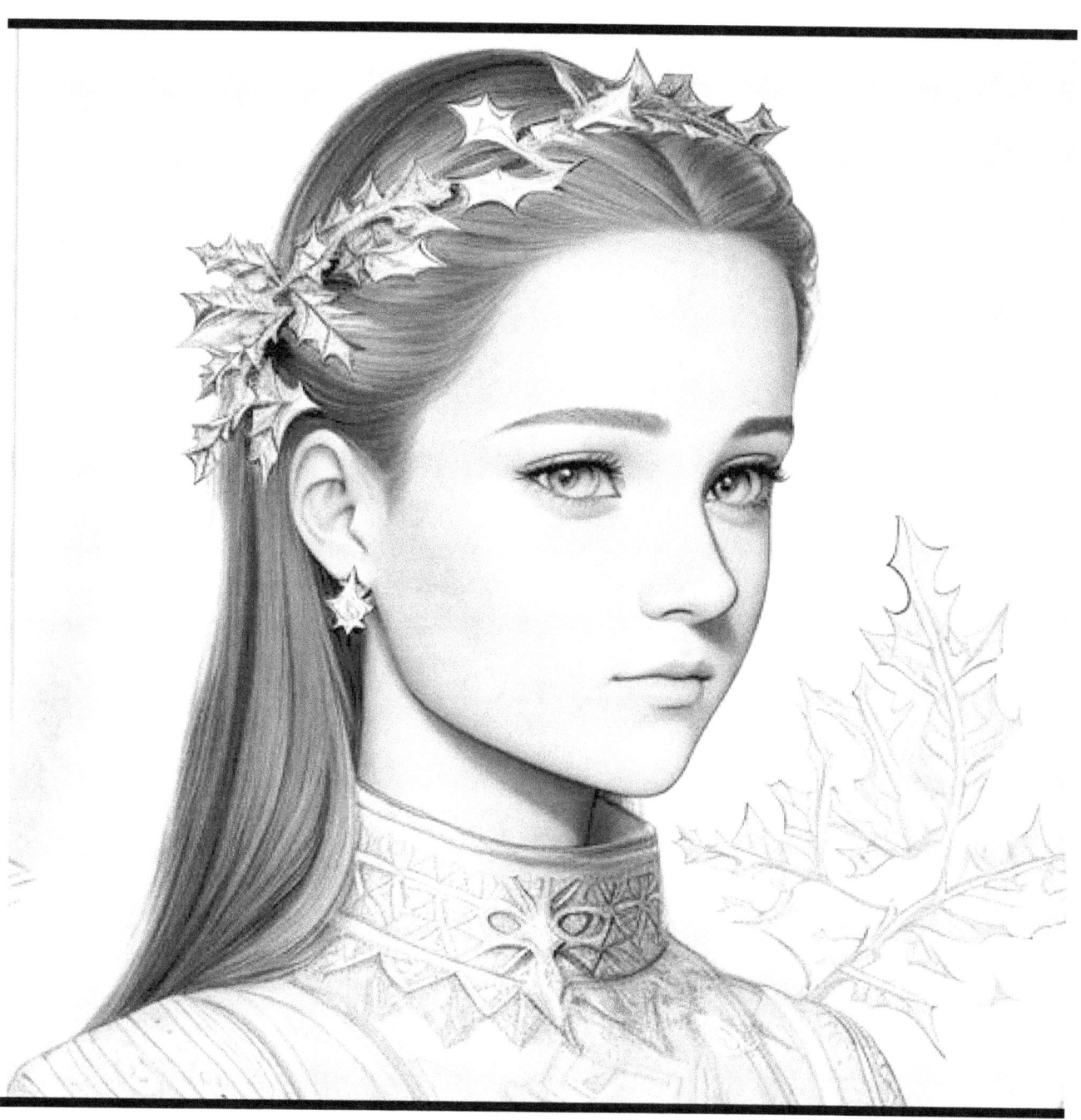

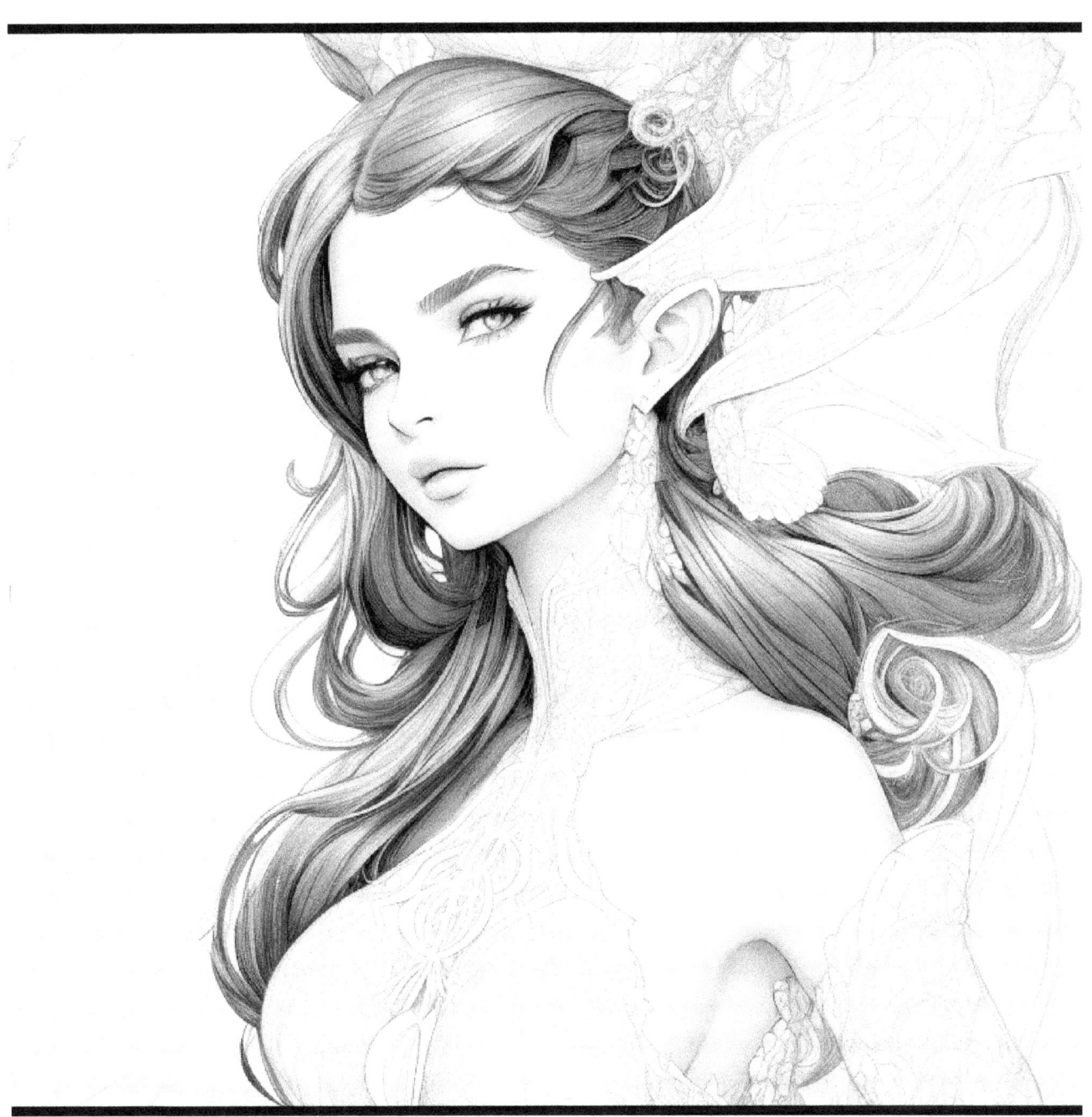

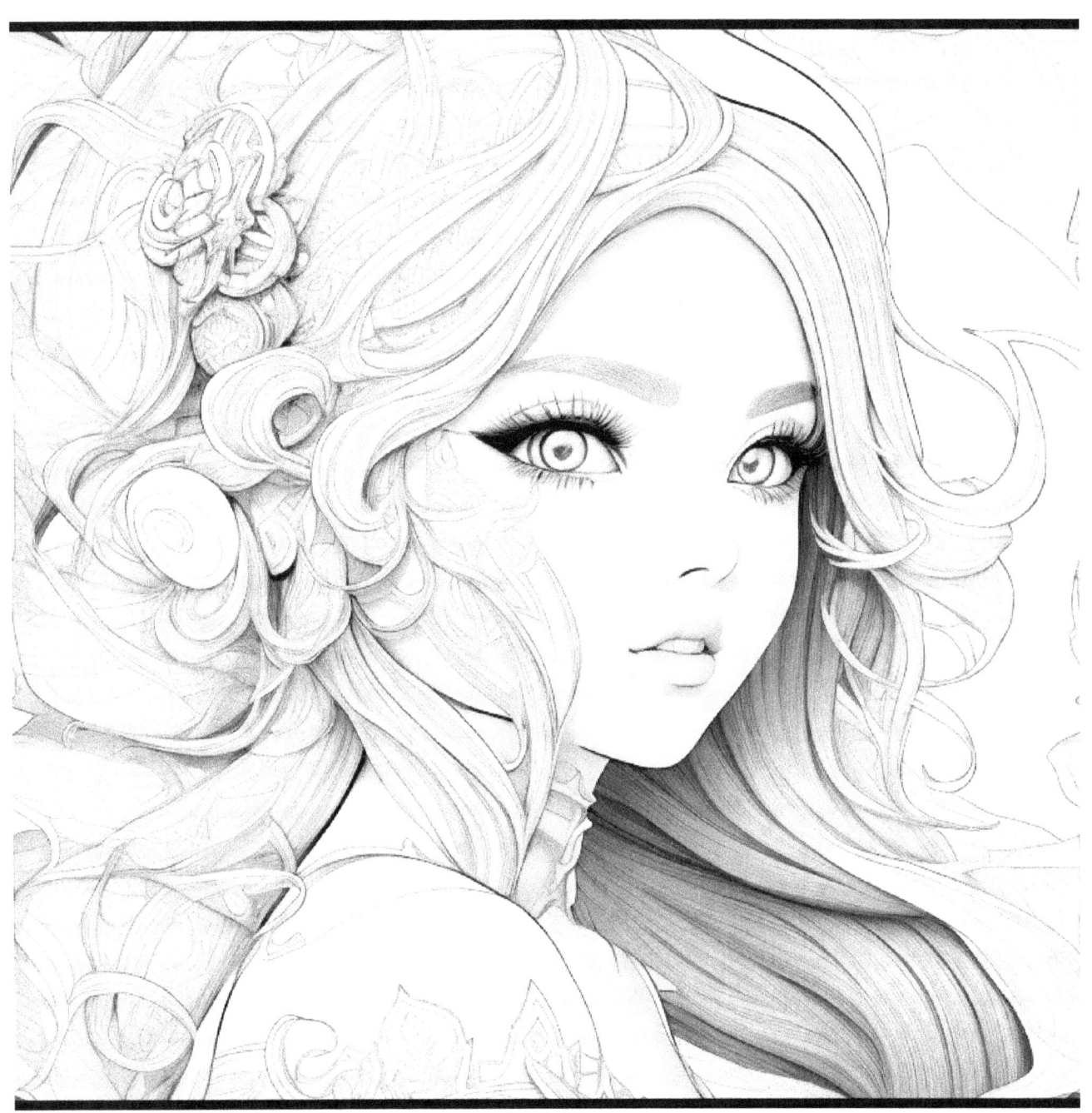

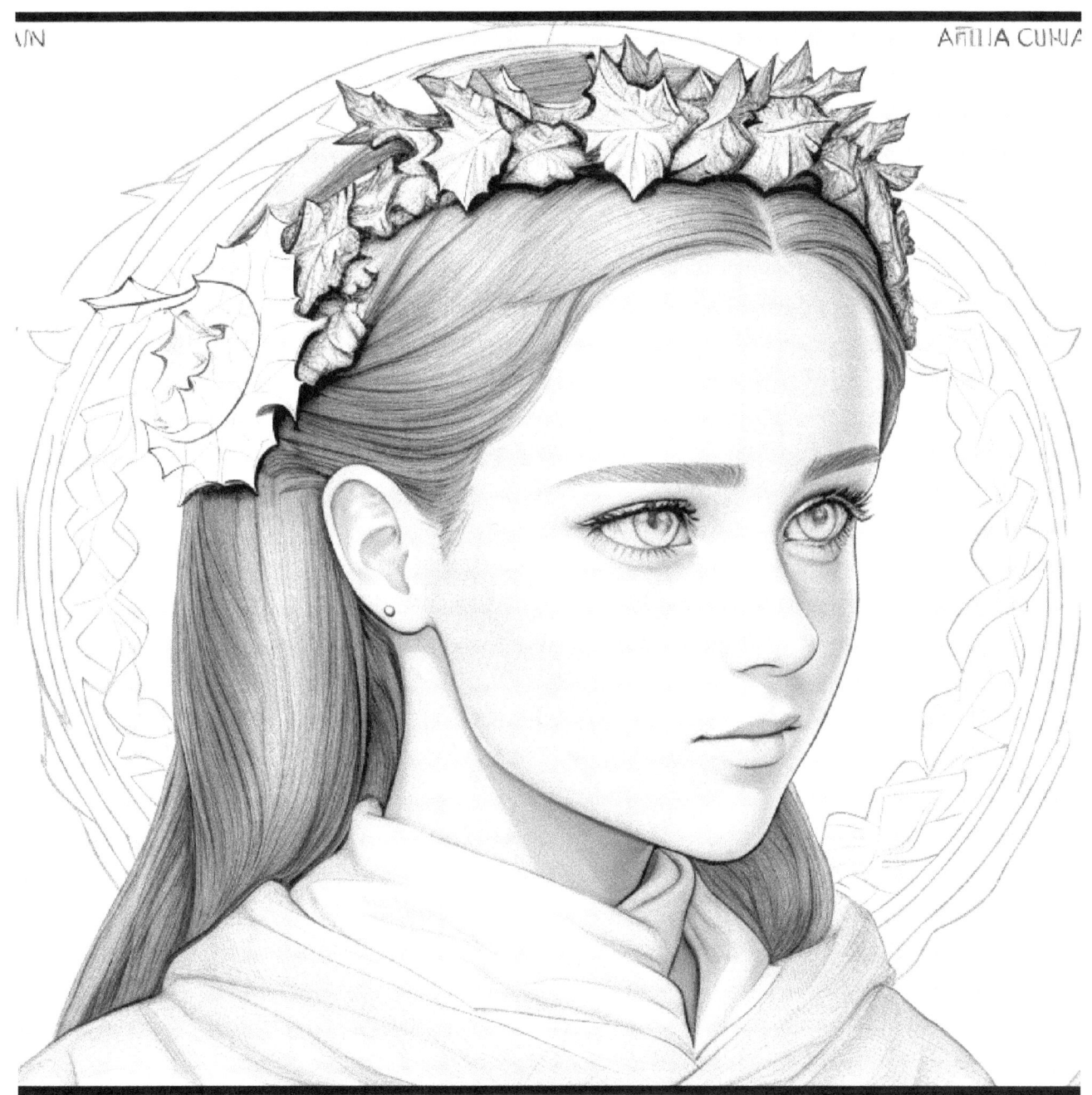

Guide Drawing

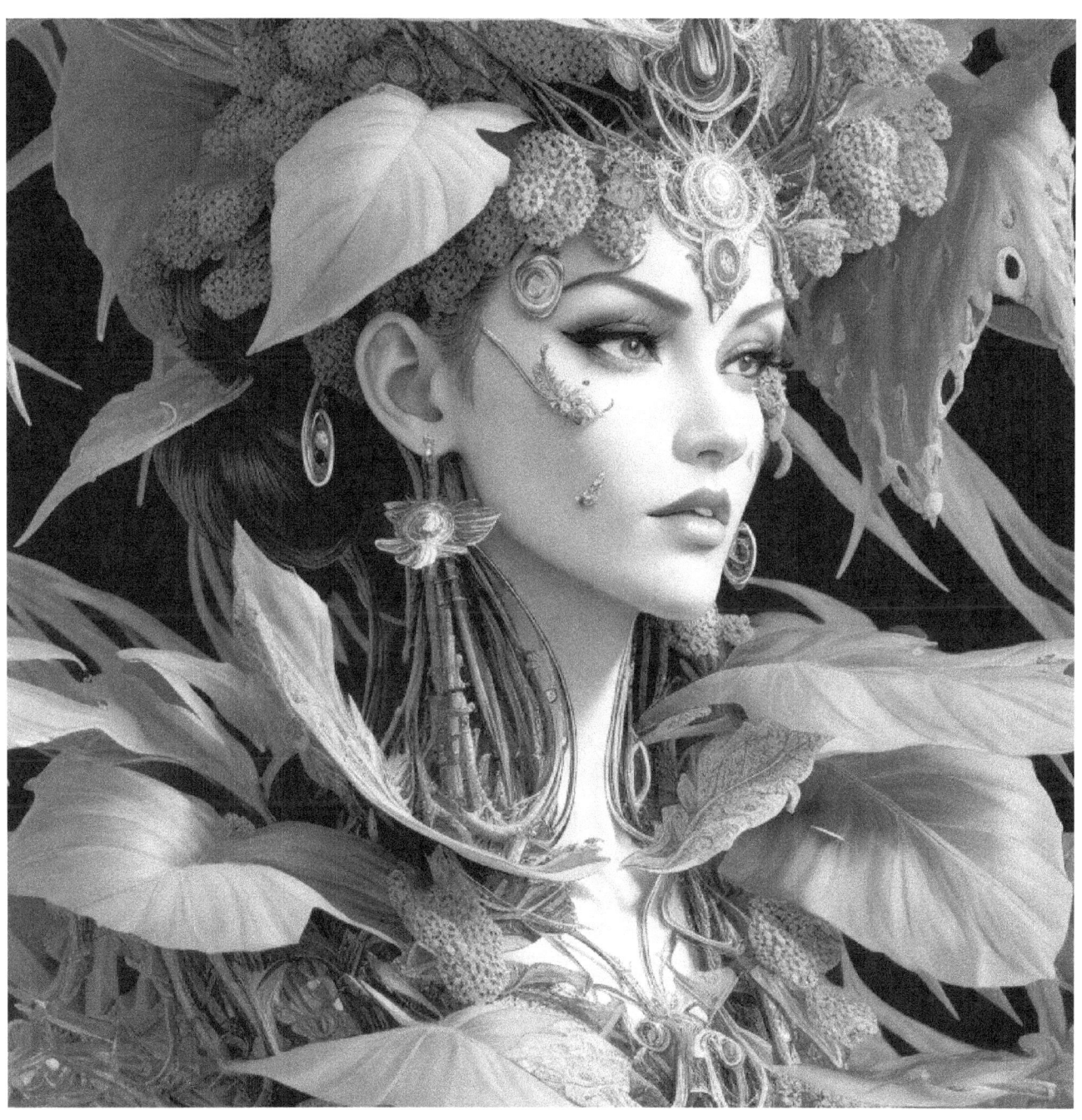

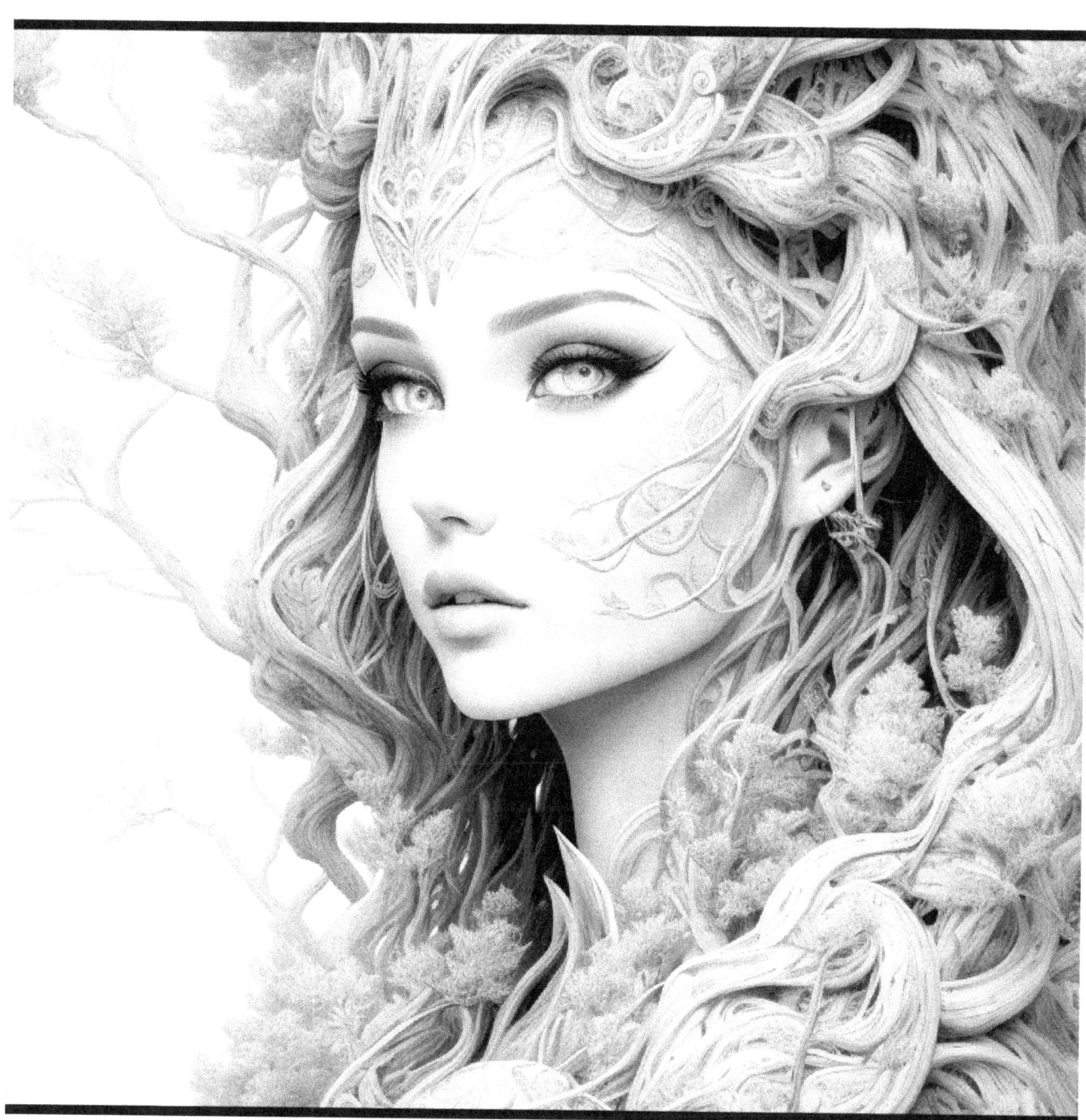

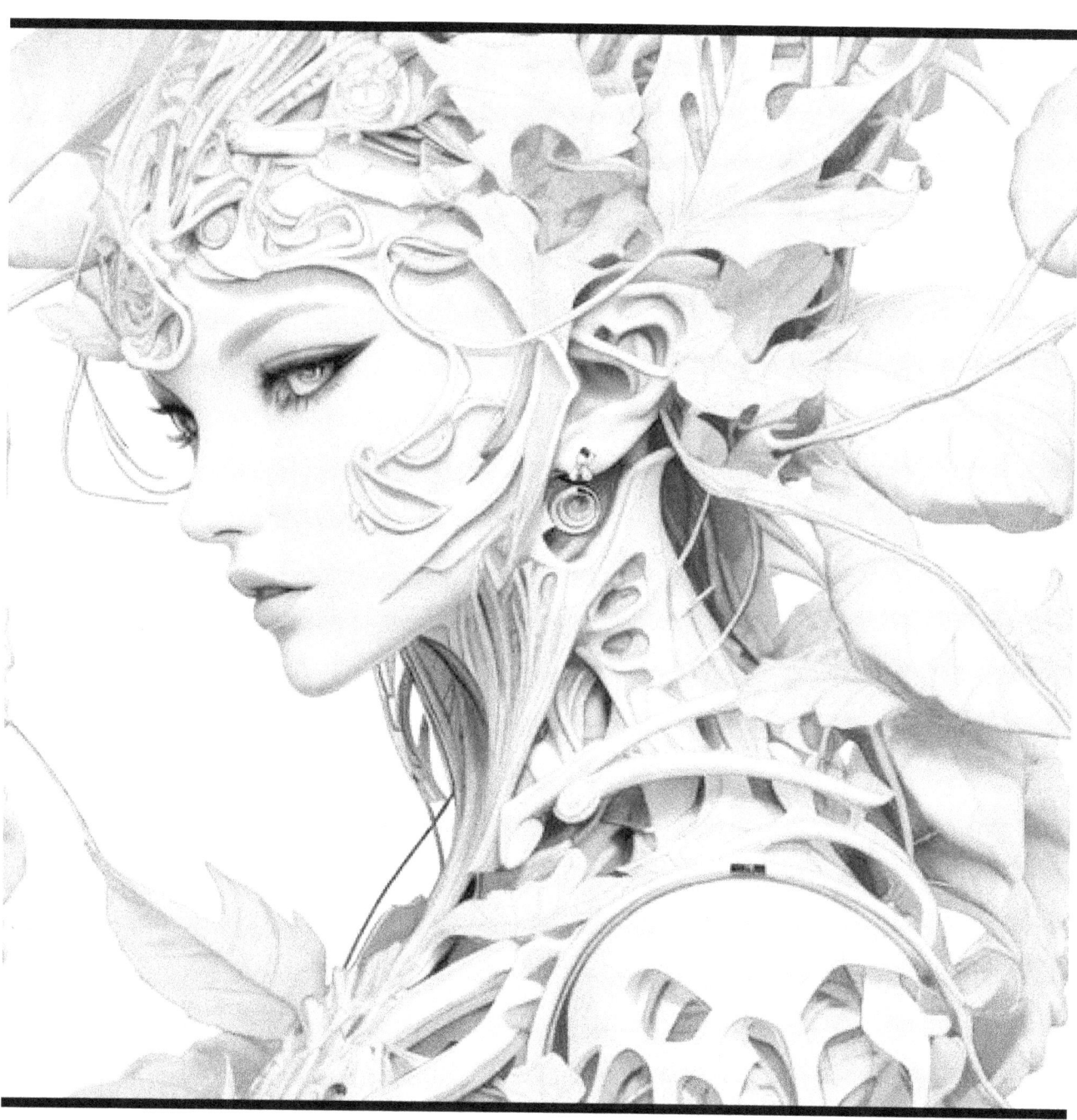

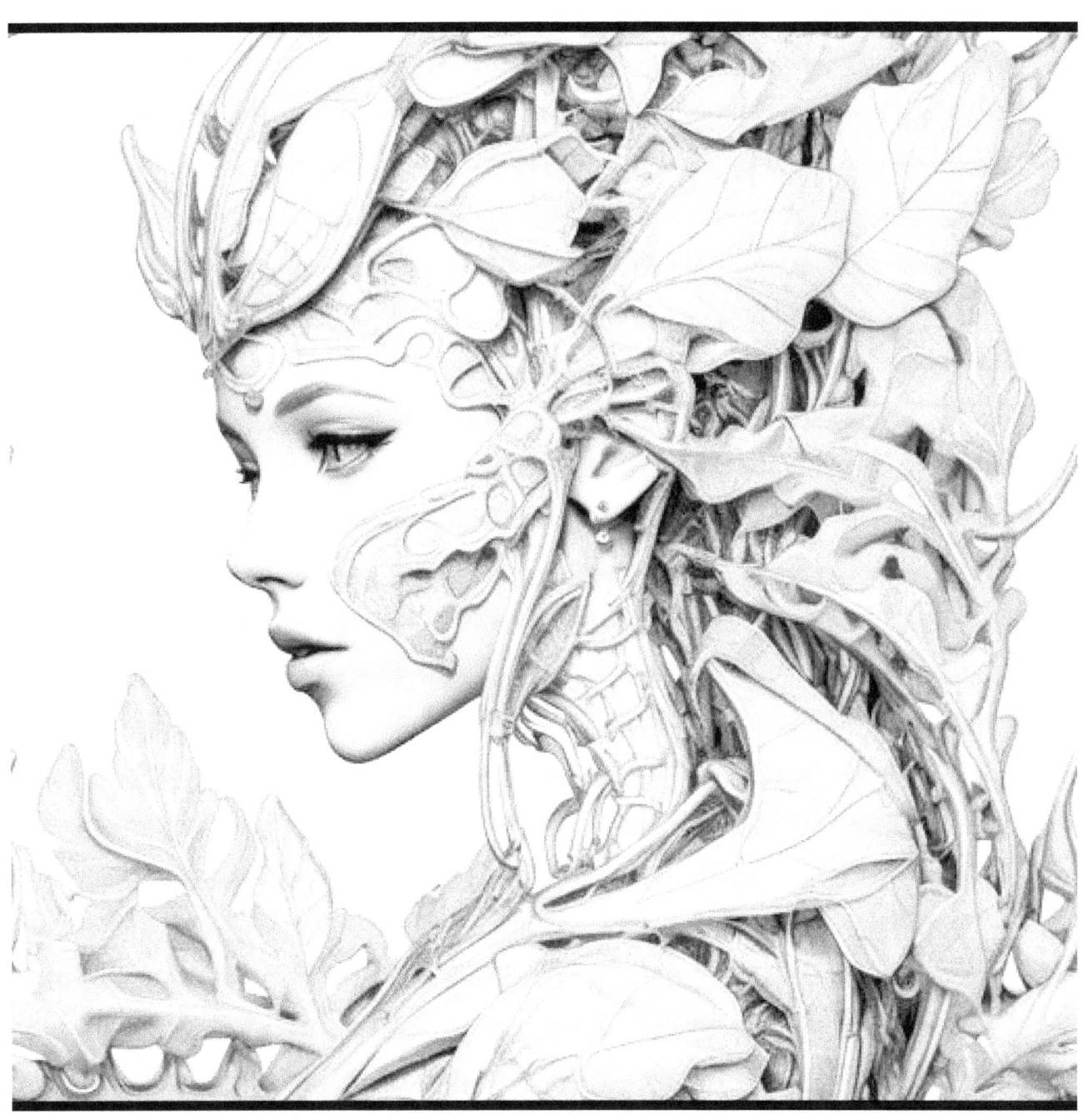

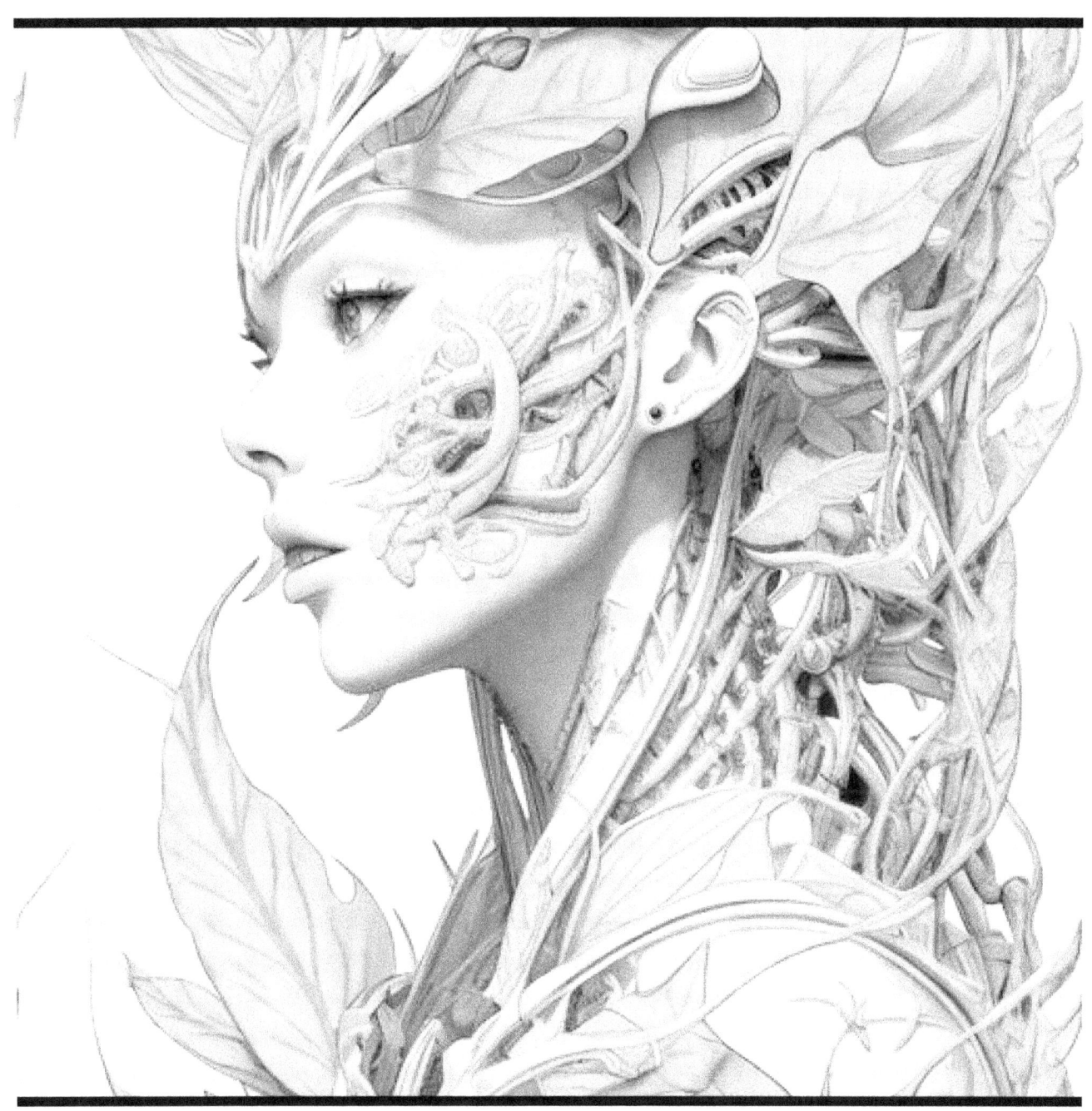

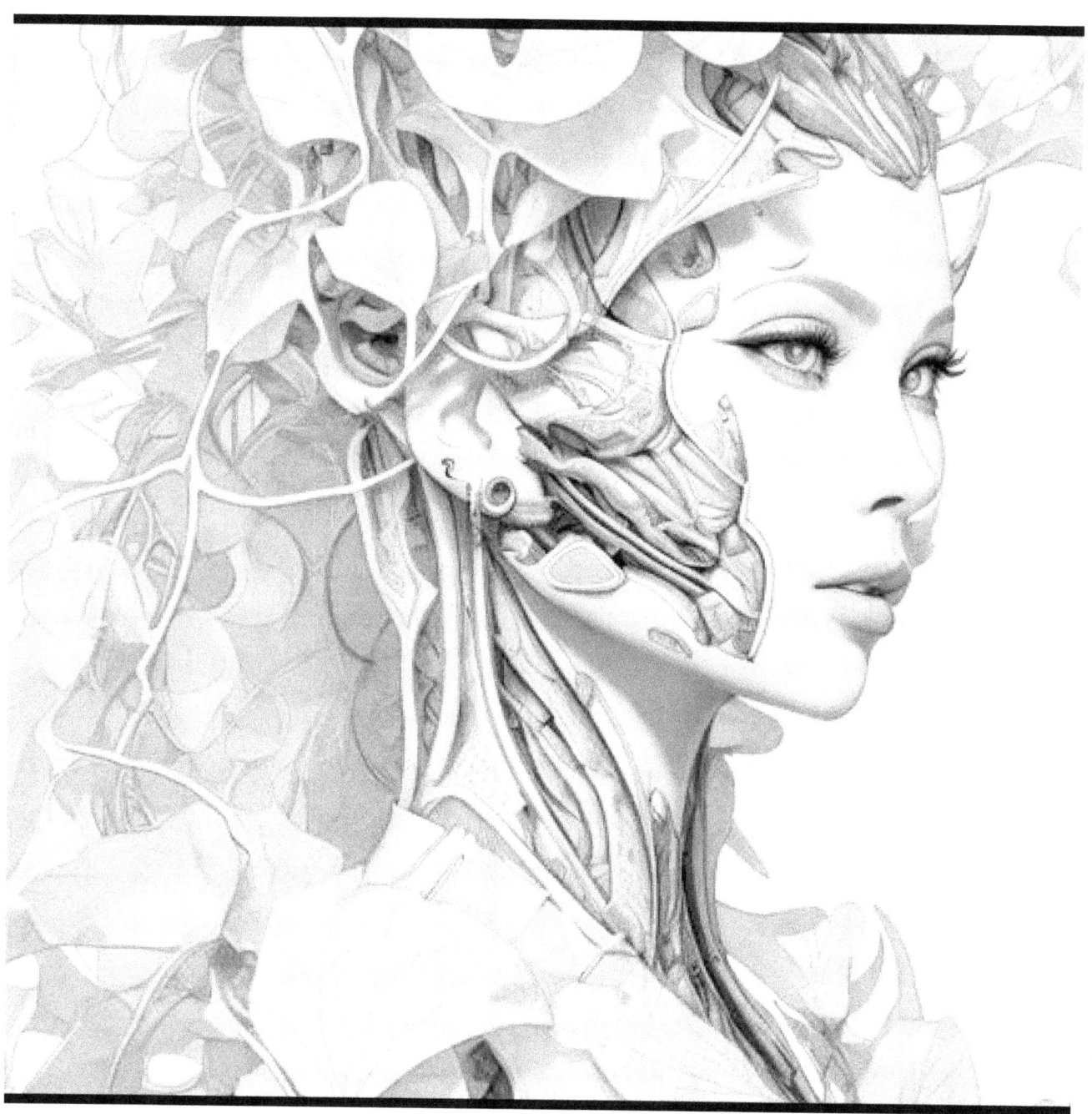

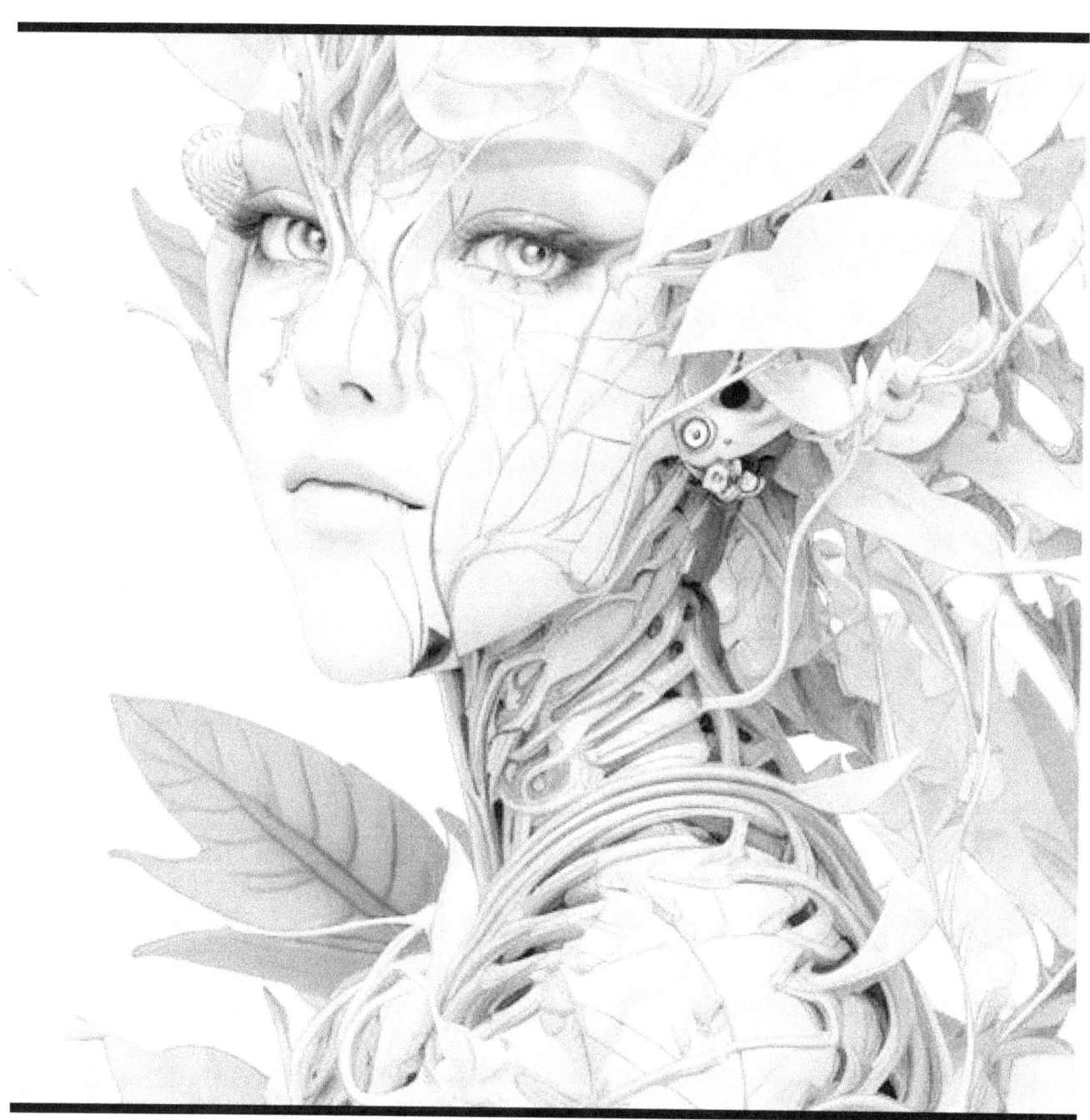

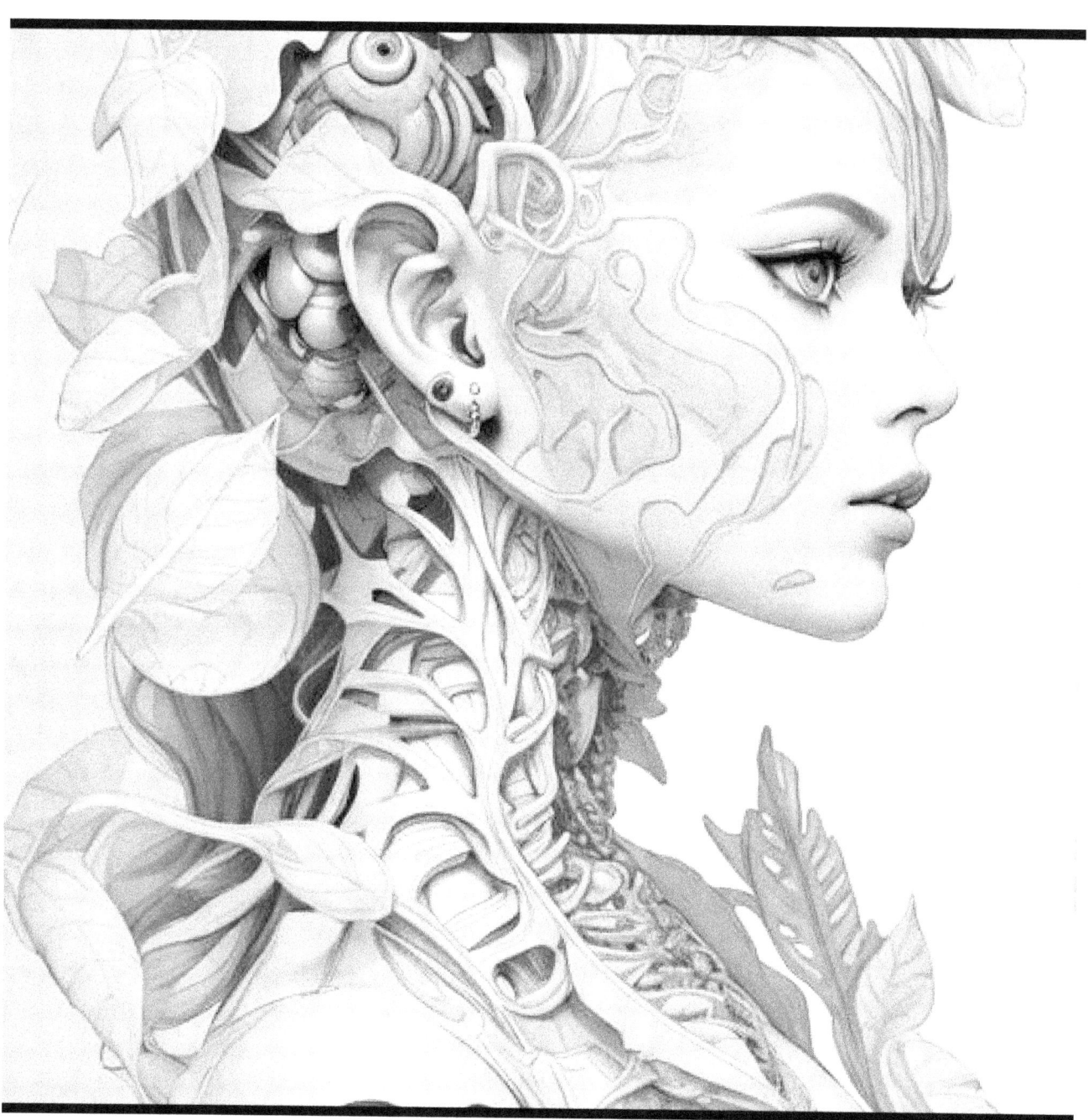

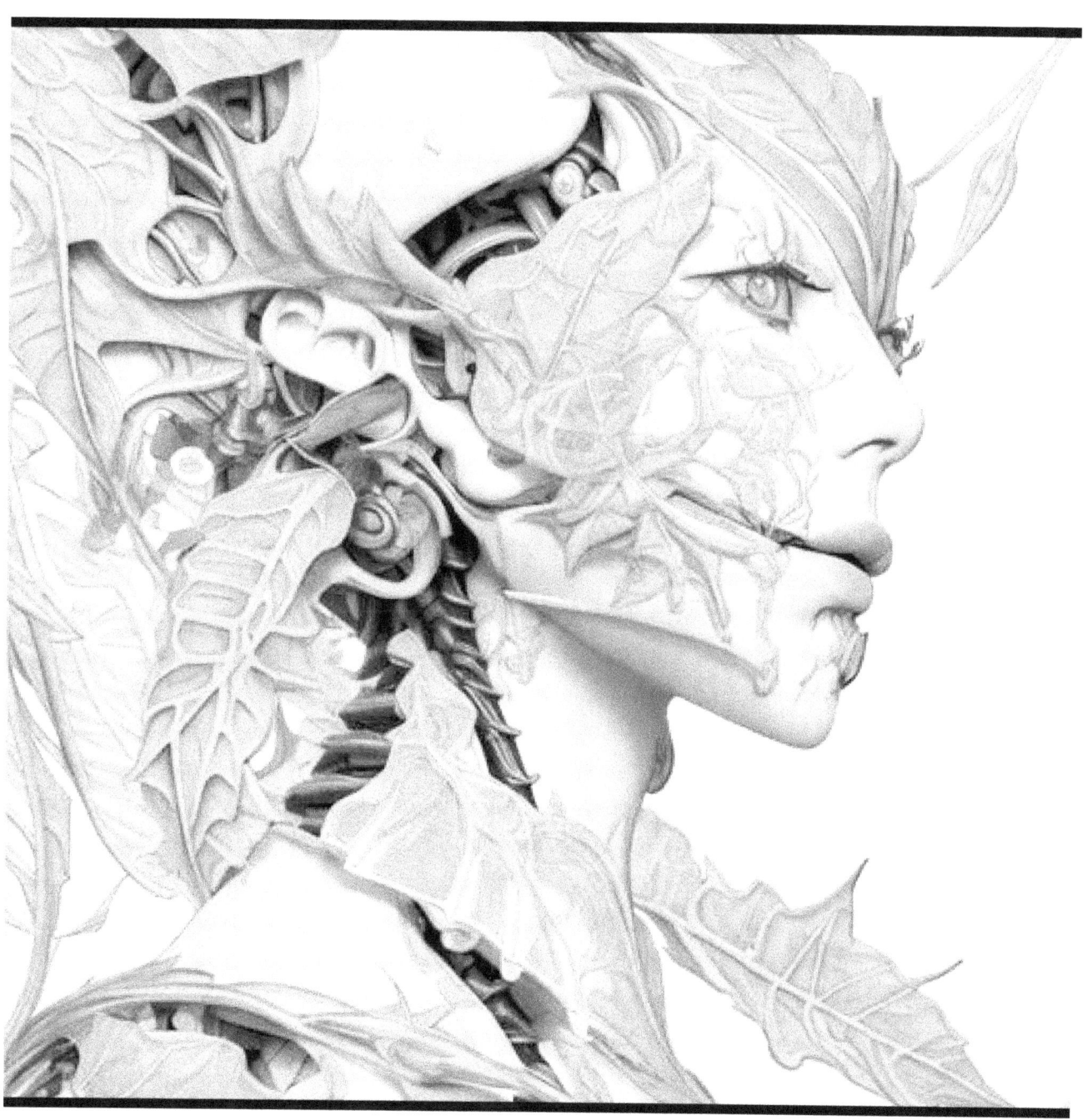

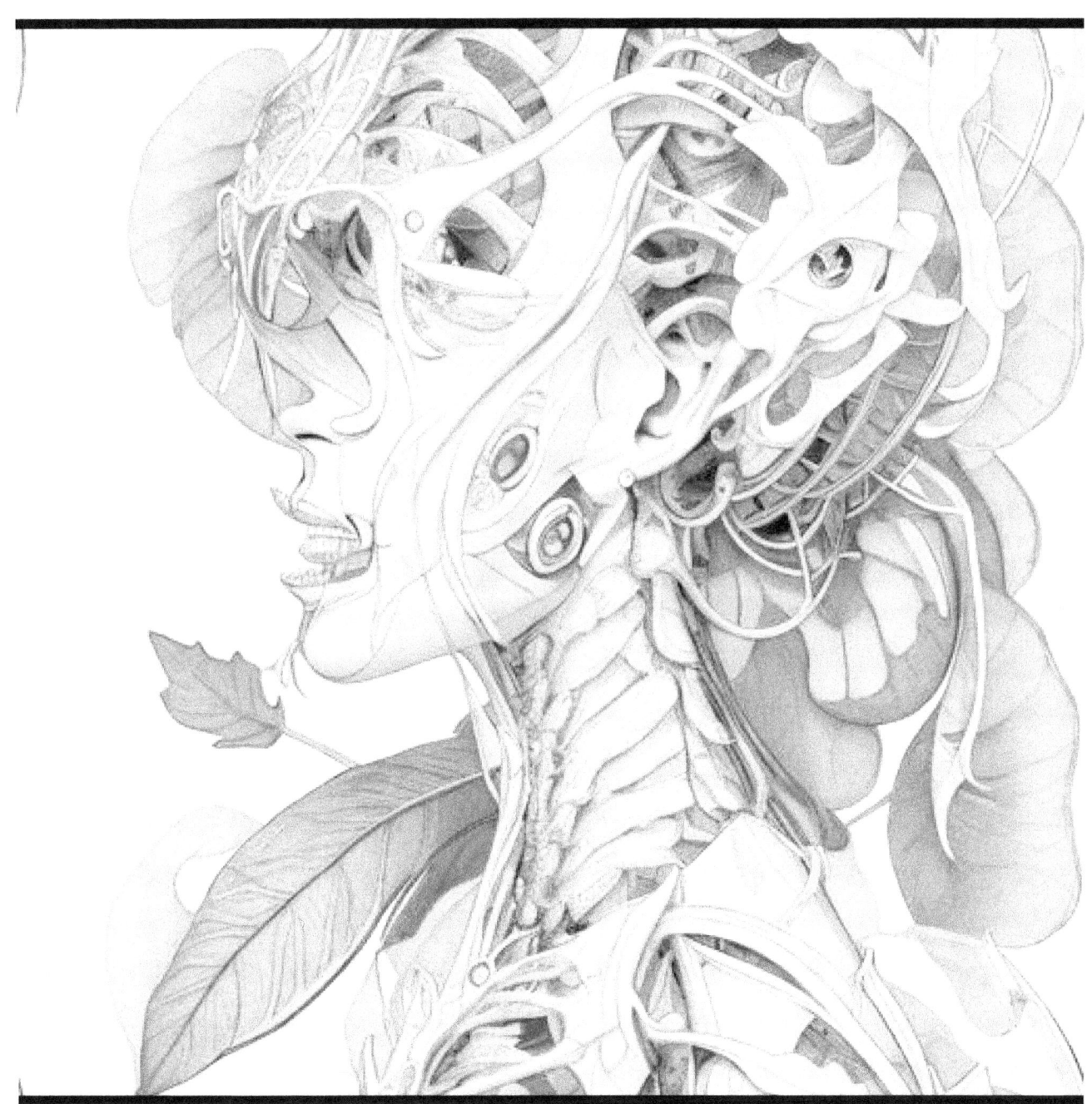

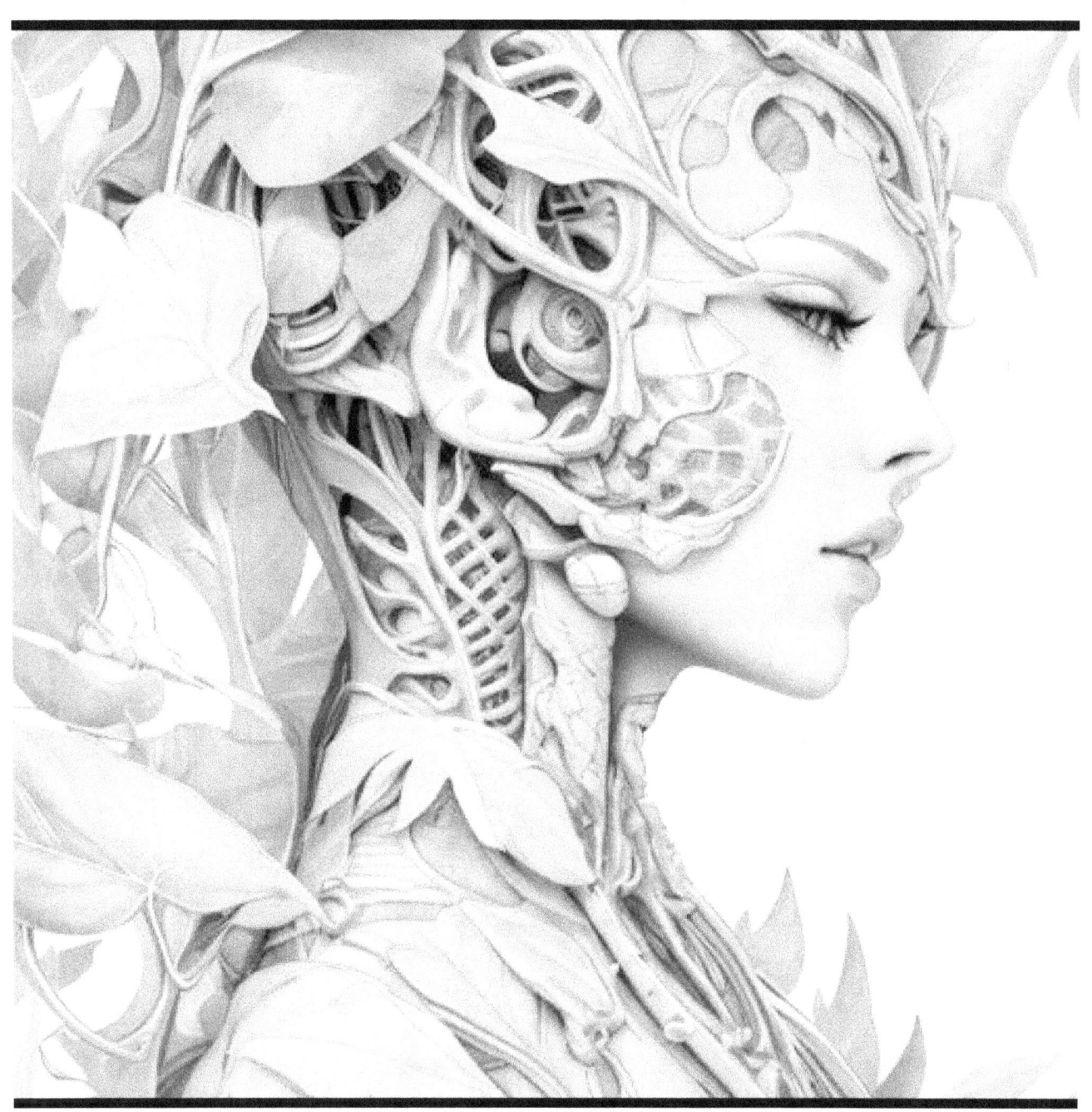

Color and pencil technique

Redraw with a fine lead pencil and
apply colors in pastel tones,
This technique will help you to
visualize a more natural contrast in
the drawings,
Enjoy making your own compositions.

Welcome to the wonderful world of fantasy adult coloring books with women's faces and medieval type nature. Enter an enchanted kingdom where beauty and magic merge on every page.

This book invites you to explore the depths of your imagination as you immerse yourself in evocative and mystical scenes. Discover the faces of empowered and captivating women, whose expressions capture the strength and wisdom of medieval times.

Each carefully designed illustration presents a combination of fantastical elements and natural landscapes that will transport you to a magical universe. Intricate details and medieval-inspired patterns will challenge you to create unique and colorful works of art.

This coloring book for adults gives you an opportunity to escape from the daily grind and immerse yourself in a state of relaxation and creativity. With every stroke of your pencil or brush, you can bring these inspiring women's faces and enchanting settings to life.